Judy Priven

EASY WRITER
BASICS TO GED

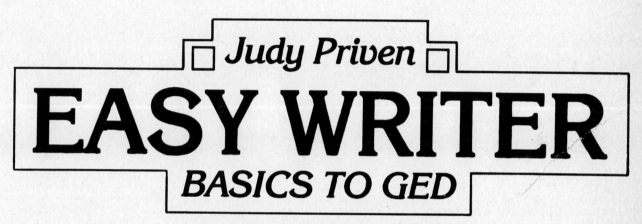

Judy Priven

EASY WRITER
BASICS TO GED

Cambridge Writing Series

CAMBRIDGE ADULT EDUCATION
Prentice Hall Regents, Englewood Cliffs, NJ 07632

Library of Congress Cataloging-in-Publication Data

Priven, Judy.
    Easy writer : from basics to G.E.D. / by Judy Priven.
        p.   cm.—(Cambridge writing series)
    ISBN 0-13-971136-8
    1. English language—Composition and exercises—Study and
teaching.   2. General educational development tests—Study guides.
I. Title.   II. Series.
LB1631.P696   1991
808'.042'07—dc20   90-22067
                                                    CIP

Editorial/production supervision
    and interior design: Shari S. Toron
Acquisitions editor: James W. Brown
Cover design: Ben Santora
Cover art: David Barnes The Stock Market
Pre-press buyer: Ray Keating
Manufacturing buyer: Lori Bulwin

 © 1991 by Prentice-Hall, Inc.
a Simon and Schuster Company
Englewood Cliffs, New Jersey 07632

Acknowledgements

Editing: Mary Bolton
        Greg Brandt

Printed in the United States of America
10 9 8 7 6 5 4 3 2

ISBN   0-13-971136-8

Prentice-Hall International (UK) Limited, *London*
Prentice-Hall of Australia Pty. Limited, *Sydney*
Prentice-Hall Canada Inc., *Toronto*
Prentice-Hall Hispanoamericana, S.A., *Mexico*
Prentice-Hall of India Private Limited, *New Delhi*
Prentice-Hall of Japan, Inc., *Tokyo*
Simon & Schuster Asia Pte. Ltd., *Singapore*
Editora Prentice-Hall do Brasil, Ltda., *Rio de Janeiro*

CONTENTS

INTRODUCTION

Is *Easy Writer* the right book for me? *Easy Writer* is for anyone learning to write. Many, but not all, use it to study for the G.E.D. You too can use this book, whether you are working by yourself or with a teacher's help—no matter how much or how little writing you have done.

What must I know before I can start *Easy Writer?* *Easy Writer* begins with easy chapters for beginning writers. This book teaches you the steps for writing a good paragraph or essay. It does not teach grammar, spelling or punctuation, so you may want to have a book or set of rules handy while you write.

Where should I begin? First, take one of the diagnostic tests. Look over your writing by yourself or with your teacher and decide which skills you need to work on. Then spend the most time with the chapters that teach those skills. If you are writing for the first time, you may not want to take a test at all; just start with the first chapter.

Are the questions in this book like those on the GED? The exercises in the first and middle chapters are easier than those on the GED—except for the CHALLENGE questions. As you go through these chapters, your writing will improve and the questions will become harder to answer. By the time you get to the last chapters, the questions will be as hard as those on tests such as the GED.

How many questions in each exercise should I do? That depends on how much time you have and how much practice you need. For example, if you have not done much writing before, you may take the time to do almost all the questions in the exercises. On the other hand, if you are just brushing up on your writing skills, you may want to answer only one question in each exercise. Even if you want to answer many questions, be sure to leave some questions for the end; after you have finished the posttest, you can use the leftover questions in each chapter for extra practice.

Will *Easy Writer* give me enough practice? *Easy Writer* lets you "dig into" the skills you need to work on. You will learn each skill step by step.

a. The EXPLANATION tells about the skills in the chapter.

b. The VOCABULARY tells what important words in the chapter mean.

c. Each skill starts with PREVIEW exercises. These exercises help you practice the skill with paragraphs or essays that are already started or written.

d. You will get the chance to write both paragraphs and essays. Because the paragraphs are shorter, they are easier to write. The essay questions get you ready for writing tests such as the GED. You can write some of the paragraphs and essays here in the book. But it is a good idea for you to keep a writing notebook. When space for writing is not provided in the book, you can write in your writing notebook.

e. In chapters 1–5, you will be given model paragraphs or essays as examples. In the other chapters, you will write the essay first and then check the model or answer in Appendix 2 (p.139–157).

f. The CHALLENGE questions at the end of many chapters are harder than the other questions in the same chapter. As the chapters get harder, the CHALLENGE questions get harder too, but none are harder than the questions on the GED.

    Decide when you will answer the CHALLENGE questions. For example, you may answer each CHALLENGE question right after you finish the chapter. On the other hand, you may want to answer all the CHALLENGE questions together, after you have gone through the whole book one time.

g. Each chapter in the first section has a **Checklist.** The **Checklist** points out the kinds of mistakes many writers make. You can avoid these mistakes by checking and correcting your work often.

How will I know when I am ready for the GED? Use the timed chapter and the posttest to decide. If you or your teacher think that you still need practice in one or more skills, go back to the chapter(s) teaching those skills. Answer any questions you did not do before. Also, try to improve the writing you did for these chapters. If you want further practice with fresh topics, there are ten additional topics in Appendix 1 (p.137).

Good writing takes time, but it can be a lot of fun—especially when your writing starts to improve. Good writing is even more fun if you talk over your ideas with a friend; both of you will learn to think more clearly while getting to know each other better. Remember—by practicing your writing and sharing your ideas, you *can* and *will* improve. *Easy Writer* shows you how to do it, but the rest is up to you!

The Diagnostic Test

The diagnostic tests will help you decide what writing skills you already have and what skills you need to work on.

The GED Rating System

When rating your test, the GED readers will consider your essay as a whole. Mainly, they will consider how well all the parts fit together to express a clear point of view. The readers of your essay may overlook one or two spelling, punctuation, or grammar mistakes. Too many mistakes, though, will take the readers' attention away from the ideas you are trying to express and thus lower your rating.

WHAT COUNTS: There are three diagnostic tests. The first tests your basic writing skills—mainly, how well your ideas are organized and how clearly they are written. The second shows whether you can write on topics of general interest and whether your ideas support your main idea. The third shows whether you can complete your essay in time and still do a good job.

WHAT DOESN'T COUNT: *Appearance*. In writing tests like the GED, the appearance of your paper does not count. You may cross out or add words and sentences to your first draft; by all means, you should correct spelling, capitalization, and other writing errors as well. Be sure that your teacher can read your essays; otherwise, you will have to write them over again.

Point of View. The questions on the GED do not have a right or wrong answer. You will not receive a low rating because the reader disagrees with what you have to say. If you can show that you have good reasons for your opinions, the opinions themselves will not matter.

How to Choose the Right Test for You

DECIDE WHICH TEST TO TAKE: Each of the three tests is for students at a different level.

- Test I is for students who are just beginning to write.

- Test II is for students who have practiced writing but are not ready for the GED.

- Test III is for students who are almost ready for the GED and who need to brush up on a few skills. This test is timed.

If you are not sure which test is right for you, look over the skills for each test and then decide.

BEFORE YOU TAKE THE TEST: Read the *skills* column; the skills listed in this column are the specific skills you should keep in mind when writing your essays.

WHILE YOU WRITE YOUR ESSAYS: Answer the question with the very best essay you can. Don't worry that your essay is "not good enough." That's why you are using this book—to get better!

AFTER YOU HAVE TAKEN THE TEST: Fill out the score column—either with a teacher or by yourself. Mark each skill with a 3, 2, or 1. A 3 means that you have mastered the skill and can move on to the next one. A 2 means that you have started to learn the skill, but need more practice. A 1 means that you have not yet started to learn the skill.

Next to the *score* column is the *chapter* column. Use these two columns to decide what chapters to work on. If you need work on all the basic skills, start at the beginning of the book and do each chapter in order. On the other hand, if your test shows that you have many writing skills, you may want to do only the chapters you need to practice.

The Posttest

After you have finished the book, take the posttest on page 129. Compare your scores with those in the diagnostic test. See how much you have improved. Then go back to the chapters you still need to practice; do any questions or exercises you did not do the first time.

DIAGNOSTIC TESTS

DIAGNOSTIC TEST   I

Directions: Write an essay that answers the question below. The essay can be as long or as short as you want.

Question: Think of all the good movies you have seen. Which was the best? Tell why you liked that movie.

_____

_____

_____

_____

_____

_____

_____

_____

_____

_____

_____

_____

_____

_____

SKILLS	YOUR SCORE	CHAPTER
a. Main idea		
answers the question	_____	2 & 3
is clearly stated	_____	3
b. Details		
are about the main idea	_____	3 & 5
do not repeat the same ideas	_____	4
c. Organization		
ideas in order	_____	5 & 6
good conclusion	_____	7 & 8
good introduction	_____	8
d. Writing		
correct sentences	_____	9, 10, 11 & 12
separate paragraphs	_____	10, 11 & 12
OVERALL SCORE	_____	

DIAGNOSTIC TEST   II

Directions: Write a 200-word essay that answers the question below. Take as much time as you want.

Question: According to one educator, almost one million American students drop out of high school every year. Do you think every adult American should try to earn a high-school diploma? Why or why not?

_____

_____

_____

_____

_____

_____

_____

_____

_____

_____

_____

_____

_____

_____

_____

_____

SKILLS	YOUR SCORE	CHAPTER
a. Main idea		
answers the question	_____	2 & 3
is clearly stated	_____	3
b. Details		
are about the main idea	_____	3 & 5
do not repeat the same ideas	_____	4
c. Organization		
ideas in order	_____	5 & 6
good conclusion	_____	7 & 8
good introduction	_____	8
d. Writing		
correct sentences	_____	9, 10, 11 & 12
separate paragraphs	_____	10, 11 & 12
e. Supporting Ideas		
specific details or examples	_____	14
good reasons	_____	15
informative		
complete		
logical		

Note: A good essay shows that you have mastered the skills listed here. If you are a *really* good writer, you may support your main idea in one of these ways:

f.	Contrast	_____	16
g.	Compare	_____	16
h.	Refute the opposite point of view	_____	17
	OVERALL SCORE	_____	

DIAGNOSTIC TEST   III

Directions: Write a 200-word essay that answers the question below. Complete the essay in 40 minutes.

Question: Children are considered a blessing by some and a curse by others. Explain the advantages and disadvantages of having children.

_____

_____

_____

_____

_____

_____

_____

_____

_____

_____

_____

_____

_____

_____

SKILLS	YOUR SCORE	CHAPTER
a. Main idea		
answers the question	————	2 & 3
is clearly stated	————	3
b. Details		
are about the main idea	————	3 & 5
do not repeat the same ideas	————	4
c. Organization		
ideas in order	————	5, 6
good conclusion	————	7, 8
good introduction	————	8
d. Writing		
correct sentences	————	9, 10, 11 & 12
separate paragraphs	————	10, 11 & 12
e. Supporting Ideas		
specific details or examples	————	14
good reasons	————	15
informative		
complete		
logical		

Note: A good essay shows that you have mastered the skills listed here. If you are a *really* good writer, you may support your main idea in one of these ways:

f. Contrast	————	16
g. Compare	————	16
h. Refute the opposite point of view	————	17
i. Complete task in time	————	18
OVERALL SCORE	————	

Chapter   1

Freewriting

Objective: to feel comfortable writing an essay

Vocabulary

freewrite— write freely; write whatever someone is thinking

☞ **Explanation:** Many people think they will never learn how to write. Some even "freeze" when they get a blank piece of paper; they simply cannot think of anything to say. This chapter is for those people. When you "freewrite," you put down whatever you are thinking; you do not worry about your ideas or about the mistakes you might make.

Picture yourself talking to a friend, either in your home or someplace where you both get together. Pretend that this person says to you:

Let's do something special this weekend. What would you like to do?

Go over in your mind how you would answer this question. Now, while your ideas are still fresh, write them down. Don't worry how your ideas will "sound" or look on the page. For now, don't worry about spelling or punctuation. Just write the words you would have spoken to your friend.

2

Chapter 1

MODEL:

> I would like to go to the beach this weekend. When we are at the beach, we could walk along the water and feel the waves. Then we could lie on the blanket and turn on my radio really loud. For lunch, we would have hot dogs, french fries, and ice cream.

Directions: Now write down what you would like to do.

_____

_____

_____

_____

_____

_____

Now pretend you are talking to a person you haven't seen in a very long time.

"What are you doing?" asks this person.

Tell a little bit about yourself. Tell about your job, your family life, the things you do to have fun.

MODEL:

> Right now I am living with my mother and brothers and sisters on Grover St. My mother doesn't work, but two of my sisters have jobs at a grocery store. My brothers still go to school.

For work, I take any little jobs I can find. My main job is loading a moving truck, but I don't like the work. The pay is good, but I don't work every day. After I pass the GED, I want to get a better job.

For fun I like to ride my motorcycle. I saved up to buy an old Yamaha RD 350 street bike. That bike really moves when it's revved up! I go so fast my girlfriend thinks I might get hurt. I'd like to learn how to fix bikes too.

Directions: Now you try it! Write down your ideas about yourself.

_____

_____

_____

_____

_____

_____

_____

_____

_____

_____

_____

_____

_____

_____

Directions: Try freewriting on any one of the following topics.

1. If you were planning the perfect vacation, where would you go? Who would you go with? What would you do once you got there?

MODEL:

> My perfect vacation would be a trip to see the wild animals in Africa. I would like to track down the lions, elephants, tigers, and zebras.
>
> Night-time in Africa would be a lot of fun. We would eat around a fire and sing songs. Then we would sleep under the stars and listen to the animals calling to each other.
>
> During the day, we would ride in a jeep. The driver could tell us all about the animals. If I learned all about the animals, maybe I could be a jeep driver too.

Now you try it:

_____

_____

_____

_____

_____

_____

_____

_____

_____

2. What is one thing that really bothers you? Tell what it is and why it bothers you so much.

MODEL:

> One thing that really bothers me is people who always think they're being cheated. Every day, at the 7-11 where I work, someone yells at me. They say I don't give them the right change.
>
> One time a guy screamed at me for giving him a dollar less than I was supposed to. He swore at me and called for the manager. When the manager went over the bill, the guy found out I had been right all along!
>
> I don't understand why people complain so much. I'm doing my best, and that's all anyone can ask.

Now you try it:

_____

_____

_____

_____

_____

_____

_____

_____

_____

_____

Directions: The questions below are hard. See if you can answer them. Write this in your writing notebook.

1. Are the people running our country doing a good job? Why or why not?

2. Suppose you could write your own TV show. Who would be the people in the show and what would they do?

Chapter 2

Understanding the Question: Paragraphs

Objective: to write a paragraph that tells what happened and why

Vocabulary

topic— what a question or sentence is about
"asking words"— words that tell you what to write

☞ **Explanation:** The first step in writing for a test such as the GED is understanding the question.

The questions in this book and on the GED have two parts: The first part tells the topic, or what the question is about. The second part tells what to write about the topic. The words telling you what to write are the "asking words."

Sample Question: What is the *best movie* you ever saw? Tell *what happened* in this movie.

MODEL ANSWER:

The best movie I ever saw was Rocky. In the movie, Rocky <u>learned how to box</u>. He became a champion.

Notice: The student has underlined the topic "best movie" and the asking words that tell "what happened."

PREVIEW

✏ EXERCISE A

Directions: Underline the topic and the "asking words" in each question below. Then write *Y* if the sentence answers the question that follows and *N* if it does not.

Hint: How can you tell if a word is part of the topic you are underlining? Try taking it out of the question. Could you still guess what the question is about? If not, the word should be underlined.

1. What is your favorite TV program? Why do you like this show?

   _____ My favorite TV program is "The Cosby Show." I like this program because the people in the Cosby family make me laugh.

2. What is one useful home appliance? Why is this appliance so useful?

   _____ One useful appliance a home should have is a refrigerator. The refrigerator keeps food fresh so we don't have to go shopping for food every day.

3. Who is one person you admire? Why do you admire this person?

   _____ One person I admire is my boss. She comes from the same home town as me.

   (*Check your answers p. 139*).

✏ EXERCISE B

Directions: Underline the topic and "asking words" in the following sentences. Then write your own sentence to answer these questions.

1. What is your favorite TV program? Why do you like this show?

   _____

   _____

   _____

   _____

   _____.

2. What is one useful appliance a home should have? Why is this appliance so useful?

_____

_____

_____

_____

_____.

3. Who is one person you admire? Why do you admire this person?

_____

_____

_____

_____

_____.

Sample Question: What was the *best movie* you have seen? Tell *why* you liked the movie.

Answers the question

The best movie I ever saw was about a woman who took care of her neighbor's baby. I liked this movie because it was so funny and true-to-life. Also, the baby was so cute that it reminded me of my little niece.

Does not answer the question

The best movie I ever saw was about a woman who took care of her neighbor's baby. Two of my friends came over and we all watched it on the VCR together. My friends all liked the movie as much as I did.

Notice: The paragraph on the right is about the topic in the question, but it does not tell *why*.

EXERCISE C

Directions: Read the following questions and answers. Underline the topic and the "asking words." Write *Y* if the paragraph answers the question. Write *N* if the paragraph does not answer the question.

1. Think of your favorite TV show. Explain why you like this show so much.

_____ My favorite TV show is "The Cosby Show." First, I like all the people in the show, even the children. Second, some of the things that happen to the children and their parents remind me of my own family when I was growing up. Lastly, the show often gives me something to think about; I learn from watching what the Cosbys do and what happens to them at the end.

2. What is one useful home appliance? Tell why it is so useful.

_____ The stove is the most useful appliance for a home to have. Of course, people can heat up food with a microwave or an electric frying pan. However, the stove is useful, too. Nowadays, most homes come with stoves already built into the kitchen.

3. Who is one person you admire? Why do you admire this person?

_____ I admire my boss. She started out as a worker like me and now she is in charge. My boss shows that people can get ahead if they work hard.

4. Think of a day in your life that you remember well. This day could be from your childhood or from your present life. Tell what happened on this day and why you remember it.

_____ I can remember the day my dog died. The whole neighborhood loved Charlie, our golden retriever. He was so friendly that no one was afraid of him, even though he was so big. After Charlie died, I didn't want to get a new dog, but finally we got a female labrador retriever. After awhile, I learned to love our new dog almost as much as Charlie.

(Check your answers p. 139).

✐ EXERCISE D

Directions: Choose three of the five following questions. Underline the topic in the first part and the words that tell *why* or tell *what happened* in the second part. Then write a paragraph in your writing notebook that answers the question.

1. What is your favorite TV show? Explain why you like this show so much.

2. What is one useful home appliance?

3. Who is one person you admire? Why do you admire this person so much?

4. What is one annoying habit that some people have? Explain why this habit is so annoying.

5. Think of a day in your life that you can remember well. Tell what happened on this day and why you remember it.

★ *Challenge Question:* What do you think is most important in life? Tell why it is so important. Write this in your writing notebook.

✔ **Checklist item:** Look over the paragraphs you wrote in this chapter. Make sure you have stated the main idea clearly in each paragraph.

Clear	Unclear
The most important thing in life is a good family. It can help if you are in trouble or need someone to talk to. It will celebrate with you when you have had some good luck or done something special. Without a good family, your sorrows seem much larger and the joys seem less important.	The most important thing in life is a good family. Most people have a family. However, not all families are good. Sometimes, parents neglect their children. Just as often, the grown children neglect their parents. The high divorce rate in this country also shows that many families are in trouble.

Chapter 3

Understanding the Question: Essays

Objective: to write an essay that tells what happened or gives reasons

Vocabulary

 essay— a piece of writing that has more than one paragraph and that has one topic

 reason— an answer that tells why

☞ **Explanation:** In this chapter, you will practice writing essays that answer different kinds of questions. An essay is a piece of writing that has two, three, or more paragraphs. These paragraphs still have only one topic.

As before, the questions in this chapter have two parts. The first part tells what the topic is, or what the question is about. The second part has the "asking words," or the words that tell you what to do. Before you begin to write, you must make sure you understand the question. Then, you will make sure that every paragraph helps to answer the question.

PREVIEW

✏️ EXERCISE A

Directions: The following question asks what happened. Read each paragraph in the answer. Write *Y* before any paragraph that answers the question. Write *N* before any paragraph that does not answer the question.

Remember: Underline the topic and the "asking words."

Question: Many people have been in trouble at one time in their lives, either as adults or as teenagers. Think of one time you were "in trouble." Tell about that time.

Essay:

a. _____ The only time I was ever in real trouble was the one time I borrowed my dad's car to get to a job interview. To tell the truth, Dad loved that car so much that I was surprised he gave me permission to drive it. Naturally, I promised to be *extra* careful!

b. _____ Everyone in the family knew how Dad loved his car. The car had a bright pink color and a convertible top. Because it was old and needed constant care, it probably wasn't worth very much money.

c. _____ On the day I borrowed the car, I was so nervous about the interview that I left the car with the keys still inside. When the job interview was over, I went out to the parking lot and started looking for the car. Suddenly, I realized it wasn't there! The car had been stolen!

d. _____ Of course, I had no choice but to call my father and explain what happened. Luckily, the police found the car on a side street an hour later. However, I never got to borrow any other car my dad owned!

(*Check your answers p. 139*).

EXERCISE B

Directions: The following questions ask you to tell what happened. Choose one of the three questions and write an essay that answers that question.

Remember: Underline the topic and the "asking words" in each question. Be sure every paragraph tells what happened.

1. Think of a time when you were so frightened that you thought you were going to die. Tell what happened at that time.

_____

_____

_____

_____

_____

_____
_____
_____
_____
_____
_____
_____
_____
_____
_____

MODEL ESSAY

1. Think of *a time when you were so frightened* that you thought you were going to die. Tell *what happened* at that time.

I can still remember the time when I was so frightened I thought I was going to die. I was driving my little Volkswagen to work and I was late. The roads were icy, but I was in a hurry. So I drove too fast.

Suddenly, the car started to skid onto the other side of the road. I saw a huge, yellow school bus coming toward me, but I couldn't stop. I just kept on sliding, right toward that bus. I just <u>knew</u> that I was going to die.

Later, I woke up in the hospital. I hurt all over, but I didn't care. I had driven my little VW into a huge bus! And I was still alive!

Notice: The beginning of the story is in the first paragraph, the middle part in the second paragraph and the end in the last one.

2. Think of one really good time you have had. Write an essay that tells what happened.

_____

_____

_____

_____

_____

_____

_____

_____

_____

_____

_____

_____

MODEL ESSAY

2. Think of one *really good time* you have had. Write an essay that tells *what happened*.

One of the best times I ever had was when I went to an amusement park with my friends. The three of us woke up at six o' clock and drove three hours to King's Dominion. We laughed and sang songs the whole way.

When we got to the park, we began going on all the rides. Of course, we only went on the scariest ones, such as the roller coaster. We all pretended to be "cool" but I was really scared each time we started to go down.

On the way home, we stopped and had pizza. I was so tired I fell asleep and didn't wake up until we got home.

3. Think of an exciting sports game you have seen. Tell what happened in the game.

PREVIEW

EXERCISE C

Directions: The following questions ask why. Read each question and essay. Write *Y* before any paragraph in the essay that answers the question. Write *N* before any paragraph that does not answer the question.

Remember: Underline the topic and the "asking words." Make sure every sentence in the paragraph answers the question.

Question: Going back to school is hard to do, especially if you are working at the same time. Tell why you decided to go back to school.

Essay:

1. _____ Going back to school is hard to do, but I'm glad I took this step. First, I hope to get a better job when I finish school. The job will pay more and I won't have to work at night.

2. _____ I also went back to school because I want to understand what my children are learning in school. I want to help them do their homework when they ask.

3. _____ Sometimes, I am too tired to go to school. I work 7 hours a day at my job. If I get overtime, I have no time to come to classes or do my homework.

   (*Check your answers*, p. 139).

EXERCISE D

Directions: Each of the following questions asks "why." Choose one of the three questions. Write an essay that answers that question.

1. Think of *one exciting sports game* you have seen. Tell *why* the game was so exciting.

MODEL ESSAY

> The most exciting sports game I ever saw was the last game of the baseball championship two years ago. The game was exciting because it decided which team would win the championship for the year.
>
> Also, the game was so exciting because it was very close. No one knew until the very end who would win.

A third reason why the game was so exciting is that both teams played so well. In the fifth inning, one of the players in the outfield caught a ball that really should have been a home run. Also, the pitchers pitched more fast balls than I have ever seen in one game.

2. Think of a place where you would like to live. Tell why you would like to live there.

3. Think of a faraway place you would like to visit. Tell why you would like to go there.

_____

_____

_____

_____

_____

_____

_____

_____

_____

_____

_____

_____

_____

★ *Challenge Question:* Think of a hard decision you have made, either this year or a long time ago. Write an essay that tells why the decision was so difficult and why you made it. Write this in your writing notebook.

✔ **Checklist:** Look over the essays you wrote in this chapter. Be sure the main idea is stated clearly in each essay.

Tells why

One of the hardest decisions I ever made was to move out of my parents' home.

One reason why this decision was so hard was the cost involved. I had to pay more rent to the landlord than I was paying my parents. Also, I had to pay for my own telephone, electricity and heat.

I wanted to move away, though, because I wanted to be on my own. I knew that my parents and I would get along much better after I had moved.

Does not tell why

When I was 23 years old, I got a job as an electrician. I started making enough money to have an apartment of my own. At that time, I was living with my parents, who liked having me there. I had a hard time deciding what to do.

Now I am living across town with my friends. Every Sunday, I take the subway and visit my parents for the afternoon. Sometimes, my dad and I watch football on TV. My mother cooks a huge meal, since she thinks I don't eat during the rest of the week.

Notice: The first paragraph of the essay on the left tells what the decision was. The second paragraph tells why the decision was hard to make. The third paragraph tells why the writer made the decision.

Chapter 4

Brainstorming:
Deciding What to Say

Objective: to "brainstorm" the outline of a paragraph

Vocabulary

"brainstorm"— to write down all your ideas

note— the most important words in an idea

☞ **Explanation:** Have you ever thought a long time about a problem? At first, you had lots of different ideas, but most of those ideas were not very good. Then, suddenly, you began to get really good ideas. You might have said, "I had a brainstorm."

The second step in the 4-step writing process is to "brainstorm" ideas. When you "brainstorm," you think of as many ideas as you can, without worrying if those ideas are good or bad. Then you write down your ideas in order to remember them. When you write down just the ideas—and not the whole sentences—you are writing notes.

Task: Write notes for the sentences below.

Steps:

1. Underline the words that tell the topic, or what the sentence is about.

2. Put the topic words in the space to the left of the sentence.

store manager

waitress

A store <u>manager</u> is the one in charge of the store.

The <u>waitress</u> meets and talks with all the <u>customers</u>.

3. Repeat with any other important words in the sentence.

store manager
in charge
waitress
meets and talks
customers

A <u>store manager</u> is the one <u>in charge</u> of the store.

The <u>waitress meets and talks</u> with all the <u>customers</u>.

PREVIEW

EXERCISE A

Directions: Read the following sentences. Write notes telling the most important ideas beside each sentence.

_____

_____

_____

_____

1. A bank teller works in a pleasant place.

2. A medic keeps people alive on the way to the hospital.

3. A park ranger explains nature to people.

4. Most truck drivers travel all over the country.

(*Check your answers, p. 139*).

Sample Question: Think of a *job* you might *like to have* in the future. Tell *what the job would be* and *why you would like it.*

Steps:

1. Underline the topic and the "asking words" in the question.

2. Think of all the jobs you might like to have. Write the names of these jobs, one under the other. Write a note that tells why.

3. Think about each job. Pick the one you want the most. Write a sentence that tells why.

MODEL ANSWER:

I would like to have the job of a store manager because I want to be in charge of a store.

EXERCISE B

Directions: Choose two of the three following questions. First, "brainstorm" your ideas; then write out the whole answer to each question.

1. Think of a job you might like to have in the future. Tell what the job would be and why you would like it.

2. What is one job you would *not* like to have? Explain why you would not like to have that job.

3. What job do you have now? Explain why you like or do not like that job. (If you don't have a job, write about someone else's or a job you had in the past.)

_____

_____

_____

_____

_____

_____

_____

_____

_____

_____

Task: Write notes that tell the most important ideas in each paragraph.

hairdresser
don't like standing
feet hurt
boss always looking

Right now, I am a <u>hairdresser</u> in a beauty shop. I <u>don't like standing</u> for so long because my <u>feet hurt</u> at the end of the day. Also, my <u>boss</u> is always looking to see if I <u>did</u> a customer's hair well.

Notice: The writer has used the topic and most important words in each sentence.

 EXERCISE C

Directions: Write notes that tell the most important ideas in each paragraph below.

1. I would like to be a house painter. This job is good for me because I like working by myself and I like making things beautiful. Another reason why I would like to be a housepainter is that I could listen to my radio all day while I worked.

_____
_____
_____
_____

2. I would like to be a teacher. One reason that teaching would be good for me is that I like helping people. Another reason is that teachers get a long summer vacation. A third reason is that teachers get a lot of respect.

_____
_____
_____
_____

3. I would like to fix cars. First, I am good with my hands. Second, I love all kinds of cars, especially sports cars. Third, I would get a good salary for fixing cars.

_____
_____
_____
_____

(Check your answers, pp. 139 & 140).

✎ EXERCISE D

Directions: Reread the sentence you wrote about a job you might or might not like in the future. Write a paragraph that gives two or three reasons why you want or do not want this job.

Notes:

_____

_____

_____

_____

Paragraph:

_____

_____

_____

_____

_____

_____

_____

_____

Directions: Write a paragraph that answers one of the two following questions. Brainstorm your answer first. Write this in your writing notebook.

1. Many people in business claim they cannot find workers to do the jobs they have. Give two or three reasons why they cannot find these workers.

2. As our country changes, people's jobs change too. What is one job that will be important in the future? Why will it be so important?

★ *Challenge Question:* What is one law you think is unfair? Write a paragraph that tells what the law is and why it is unfair. Write this in your writing notebook.

✔ **Checklist:** Look over the paragraphs you wrote in this chapter. Make sure that you did not repeat the same idea in different words.

Different ideas	Same ideas
I would like the job of a store manager. I like helping people decide what to buy. Also, I am good at making sure that other people, such as the cashiers, do their jobs.	I would like the job of a store manager. The job of a store manager would be good for me. I want to be in charge of a store.

Notice: Look at the paragraph on the right-hand side. The second and third sentences in the first paragraph repeat the idea in the first sentence.

Chapter 5

Organizing Your Ideas

Objectives: to write headings for groups of details and to write an essay based on groups of details

Vocabulary

    title— name for all the ideas in a list
    heading— name for one group of ideas in a list
    detail— an idea that tells part of the main idea
    relevant— having to do with the main idea

 Explanation: Another important part of brainstorming is organizing your ideas. When you organize ideas, you decide what ideas should go together, or be put in the same group. Giving a name, or heading, for each group of ideas is important because it helps you write what each group is about.

Task: Decide what ideas, or details, should be grouped together. Then find the heading for each group.

Steps:

1. Read the title at the top; these words tell you what the word list is about. Then read through the whole list to see the details.

2. Put "a" beside the first note. Then, put "a" beside all the notes that go with the first one. If you are unsure about a note, do not put a letter beside it.

3. Start at the top of the list again. Put "b" beside the first word that has no letter. Put "b" beside all the other ideas that go with that one.

4. Go back and put a letter beside any ideas you left out.

Job of a Store Manager

    a interview people to work in store

    a hire new workers

    b check to be sure the shelves are full

    b order new items when needed

    a advertise jobs in newspaper

    b keep store supplied

5. Look over all the ideas with "a" beside them; draw a line under the heading for those words. Then draw a line under the heading for the "b" words.

Job of a Store Manager

    a interview people to work in store

    a <u>hire new workers</u>

    b check to be sure enough items are on shelves

    b order new items when needed

    a advertise jobs in newspaper

    b <u>keep store supplied</u>

6. Write each group of details beside the right headings.

Job of a Store Manager

a. hire new workers — interview people who want to work in store, advertise jobs in newspaper

b. keep store supplied — order new items when needed, check to be sure enough items are on shelves

PREVIEW

EXERCISE A

Directions: Group the details in the following lists and write a heading for each group.

1. City Living

   smog
   many movies and comedy clubs
   different kinds of jobs
   disadvantages
   heavy traffic
   good shopping malls
   advantages
   crime

2. Changes Caused by Technology

   home
   VCRs
   fax machines
   compact disk players
   office computers
   business
   microwave ovens

_____

_____

_____

_____

_____

_____

_____

_____

_____

_____

_____

_____

_____

(*Check your answers, p. 140*).

Task: Put the details below into groups and write a heading for each group.

1. Read through the whole list.

2. Put *a*, *b*, or *c* beside each detail as you did above.

   Title: Benefits of Saving

   a money in case I get sick

   b interest

   c downpayment on car

   a money in case I lose job

   c downpayment on house

3. Think of a heading for each group of details; the heading should tell the way in which all the details in that group are alike

   Benefits of Saving

   Emergency money
      sickness
       lose jobs
   Interest
   Downpayments
      car
       house

EXERCISE B

Directions: Choose two of the following lists. Write two or three headings for each list and group the details underneath.

1. Having Your Own Business

   can give people you know jobs
   don't have job benefits
   need money to start out
   lose money if business fails
   can decide where and when to work

2. Modern Problems

   dirty water
   smog

acid rain
homelessness
hunger
oil spills
not enough good jobs

3. Job of a Parent

feed child healthful foods
help child with homework
keep child warm in winter
listen to child's problems
teach child right from wrong
give child a place to sleep
play games with child
take child for checkups at the doctor's

_____

_____

_____

_____

_____

_____

_____

_____

_____

_____

_____

_____

_____

(*Check your answers, p. 140*).

EXERCISE C

Directions: Choose one set of the previous notes. Use the notes to write a paragraph.

_____

_____

_____

_____

_____

_____

_____

_____

_____

Directions: Choose one of the two following questions. Brainstorm your ideas for an essay that answers this question. Then write headings for your ideas.

Hint: Use the same steps as above. Write a separate paragraph for each heading and group of details.

1. Think of a special occasion, such as a party you have had or a holiday you have celebrated. How important are birthdays, parties, and holidays? Explain why you think the way you do.

2. Scientists say that our daily lives are changing more quickly than ever before. Describe the changes in daily life since you were born.

_____

_____

_____

_____

_____

_____

_____

_____

_____

_____

_____

_____

_____

_____

_____

★ *Challenge Question:* Imagine what daily life will be like in 20 years. Write an essay that describes the ways in which life will change from the way it is now. Write this in your writing notebook.

✔ **Checklist:** Look over the essays you wrote in this chapter. Make sure that every idea is relevant, or says something about the main idea.

Relevant	Not relevant
Life in America has changed a lot in the last twenty-five years. Twenty-five years ago, most women stayed at home to cook and to raise their children; today, most women work out of the home and earn money to help the family. Twenty-five years ago, people were not as worried about drugs as they are today. In some ways, our lives have improved, but in other ways our lives have gotten worse.	Life in America has changed a lot in the last twenty-five years. Twenty-five years ago, people were not as worried about drugs as they are today. Of course, some people still don't realize how much of a problem drugs are and how much crime it is causing. They also don't care how much our children are learning in school. In some ways, our lives have improved, but in other ways our lives have gotten worse.

Notice: The main idea of both paragraphs is stated in the first sentence. The underlined sentences in the right-hand paragraph are not about this idea.

Chapter 6

Putting Your Ideas in Order

Objectives: to put ideas in order of their importance and to write essays with the ideas ordered according to their importance

Vocabulary

order— decide what comes first, second, etc.

 Explanation: In this chapter, you will finish brainstorming your ideas by putting them in order; in other words, you will decide which ideas should come first, second, third, or fourth.

One way to order your ideas is to start with the most important ones. In this way, you make the reader pay attention right away.

Sample Question: Many people would like to live outside a big city. Think of the advantages of living outside the city. Explain what these advantages and disadvantages are.

MODEL ANSWER:

Living outside a big city has many advantages. The main advantage is that living outside the city does not cost as much as living inside the city. For example, homes are cheaper to buy or rent. Also, the taxes are not as high.

The next biggest advantage of living outside the city is that there is less crime. People are not afraid to take a walk at night or to let their children out to play.

One last advantage to living in the suburbs or in the country is that there is more room. The houses are bigger and the streets are not as crowded.

Notice: Words such as *main*, *biggest*, and *last* tell the reader how important each idea is.

PREVIEW

EXERCISE A

Directions: Number the paragraphs according to how important the author says they are. Then, draw a line under any words that tell how important each idea is.

Hint: Underline words such as "mainly" and "also."

1. *Question:* Pretend you are President of the United States. What changes would you make in our country? Explain each change.

   _____ Another important change I would make is to help people find homes. Many people live in the streets because they have nowhere to go. The government should build more places where these people can sleep and eat.

   _____ If I were President, I would make many changes. Mainly, I would help people find good jobs. I would pay people to work if they could not find a job on their own.

   _____ A third change I would make is to help working people find a place for their children. Many day care centers are too crowded. Some cost more than people can pay.

   (*Check your answers, p. 141*).

2. *Question:* Pretend you suddenly won the lottery and became a millionaire. How would your life change as a result? Describe these changes in order of their importance.

   _____ Also, if I had a million dollars, I would go on vacations around the world. Even though I have never been in an airplane, I'm sure that I would enjoy visiting other parts of the country, especially Alaska.

   _____ The most important way in which my life would change is that I would move into a larger home in a different part of town. Right now, my apartment is so small that the baby sleeps in the same room as my wife and me. Also, I am afraid to go out at night because of the crime.

   _____ Secondly, I would retire from work. Instead of going to the factory every day, I would do whatever I wanted. For example, I might go bowling or just stay home and watch TV.

   (*Check your answers, p. 141*).

✏ EXERCISE B

Directions: Choose three of the following four questions. Write an essay that answers the question. Order your ideas according to how important they are.

1. Think of the best vacation you have ever had. List in order of their importance the reasons why this vacation was so good and explain each reason. After you have completed your answer, compare it with the model on p. 141.

_____

_____

_____

_____

_____

_____

_____

_____

_____

_____

_____

_____

_____

2. Pretend you are the boss where you work. What changes would you make? List these changes in order of their importance and explain each change. After you have completed your answer, compare it with the model on p. 141.

_____

_____

_____

_____

_____

_____

_____

_____

_____

_____

_____

_____

_____

_____

3. Do you prefer to rent or to own your home? List the reasons for your answer in order of their importance and explain each reason.

_____

_____

_____

_____

_____

_____

_____

_____

_____

_____

_____

_____

4. Pretend you are a millionaire. Write an essay that describes how your life would change. Be sure to order your ideas according to their importance.

_____

_____

_____

_____

_____

_____

_____

_____

_____

_____

_____

_____

_____

_____

Directions: Review the paragraphs you wrote in the chapter before this one. Rewrite the paragraphs so that their ideas are ordered according to their importance. Write this in your writing notebook.

★ *Challenge Question:* In what ways has your life changed in the last few years? Write an essay that explains these changes in the order of their importance. Write this in your writing notebook.

✔ **Checklist:** Go over each essay you wrote in this chapter. Be sure that no ideas are in the wrong place.

Right place	Wrong place
My job as a mail person in a big office building has many advantages.	My job as a mail person in a big office building has many advantages.
The most important advantage is the good pay. For the first time in my life, I am able to save money for a new car or even for a house.	One important advantage is the fact that I meet everyone in the building when I deliver the mail. Most of the people are friendly and like to chat about sports or the weather.
Almost important as the pay are the job benefits. For example, I don't have to worry that someone in my family might get sick; my health insurance will pay for most of the expenses.	The most important advantage is the good pay. For the first time in my life, I am able to save money for a new car or even for a house.
A third advantage is the fact that I meet everyone in the building when I give out the mail. Most of the people are friendly and like to chat about sports or the weather.	Almost important as the pay are the job benefits. For example, I don't have to worry that someone in my family might get sick; my health insurance will pay for most of the expenses.

Notice: The first essay states the most important idea first. The second essay states the most important idea in the middle.

Chapter 7

Writing Conclusions:
Paragraphs

Objective: to write a paragraph with a good introduction and conclusion

Vocabulary

> introduction— first part of a paragraph or essay
> summarize— tell what is in the paragraph
> conclusion— overall idea at the end

☞ **Explanation:** The next step in the writing process is to write your paragraph or essay. The first and last parts of the paragraph or essay are often the hardest to write.

Many good writers start with the most important idea, or the main idea; this is the introduction. The ending, or conclusion, ties all the ideas together.

The conclusion of a paragraph can

- summarize the paragraph, or tell what the paragraph or essay says about the main idea.

- tell how a problem should be solved.

- tell what will happen in the future.

Note: You can use any type of conclusion for essays on writing tests such as the GED.

PREVIEW

✏ EXERCISE A

Directions: Read each paragraph below. Label each conclusion in the space before the last sentence. Write:

a. "SU" if the conclusion summarizes the paragraph, or tells what it says about the main idea.

b. "SO" if the conclusion tells how a problem should be solved.

c. "F" if the conclusion tells what will happen in the future.

1. *Question:* Think of one problem that many people have. Give one or more reasons why the problem exists.

   Paragraph: Many people have a problem because they can't find a good place to live. First, some people do not have enough money to pay the rent. Second, most cities do not have enough places for people to live in. Third, many landlords don't paint the walls or fix things that are broken.

   Conclusion 1: _____ These reasons show why finding a good home can be a problem.

   Conclusion 2: _____ Cities should build more homes and let people buy them at a low price.

   Conclusion 3: _____ If our cities don't have good housing soon, more and more homeless people will be in the streets.

   (*Check your answers, p. 141*).

2. *Question:* What is the meaning of the saying "Nothing ventured, nothing gained?" Give an example that explains why this saying is true.

   Paragraph: "Nothing ventured, nothing gained" means that people who don't take chances won't get what they want. For example, I took a chance when I left home and moved to this city. I didn't know anyone here, so I was afraid I would be lonely. Once I moved here, I made new friends. I also got a better job than I would have had at home.

Conclusion 1: _____ *This example shows how taking a chance made me happier than before.*

Conclusion 2: _____ *If people would take more chances, they might improve their lives.*

(*Check your answers, p. 141*).

✏️ EXERCISE B

Directions: Write a conclusion for each of the paragraphs below.

Hint:

    a. To write a conclusion that summarizes, use the word "reasons" or "examples."

    b. To write a conclusion that solves a problem, use the word "should" or "must."

    c. To write a conclusion that tells about the future, start with the word "if."

1. *Question:* Think of one problem many workers have. Explain what the problem is. Give at least one example to show what you mean.

   Paragraph: One problem many workers face is lack of safety. Most people know that jobs like those of the police and firefighters can be dangerous. However, many other kinds of workers—such as timber cutters, coal miners, and electricians—may get hurt in accidents. Others have to work with fumes or materials that may cause sickness.

   Conclusion:

   _____

   _____

   _____

   _____

2. *Question:* We often use the phrase "common sense." Write a paragraph that tells what "common sense" is. Give at least one example to show what you mean.

    Paragraph: "Common sense" is what people know from their own experiences. For example, people who want to lose weight don't need a doctor to tell them not to eat ice cream; they just need to use "common sense," or what they know from other diets. In the same way, most people don't need an expert to tell them which car they can afford; by now, they know that if they pay too much money for a car, they won't have enough later on.

    Conclusion:

    _____

    _____

    _____

    _____

3. *Question:* Yogi Berra, the famous baseball pitcher, once said, "It's not over 'til it's over." Explain what Berra meant.

    Paragraph: When Berra said, "It's not over 'til it's over," he meant that a team could never be sure it had won the game until the very end; a team that is far ahead in the beginning can still lose in the ninth inning. This saying is true even outside the ballpark. For example, people who start out without much money can work hard and do well in the end.

    Conclusion:

    _____

    _____

    _____

    _____

EXERCISE C

Directions: Choose two of the following three questions. Write a paragraph that answers each of the questions you have chosen. The first sentence of each paragraph will tell the main idea; the last sentence will be the conclusion. Be sure to brainstorm your ideas first. Write this in your writing notebook.

1. Think of any problem you or someone you know has had. Describe this problem and tell why it was important.

2. Think of a problem many parents have when they are raising children. Describe this problem and tell how it can be solved.

3. Think of an important problem many workers face. Explain what the problem is. Give at least one example to show what you mean.

★ *Challenge Question:* Explain what you think is the most important problem the country faces. Write this in your writing notebook.

✔ **Checklist:** Look over each paragraph you wrote in this chapter. Make sure that the conclusion goes with the other sentences in the paragraph.

Good conclusion	Poor conclusion
I faced a *personal problem* when I worked as an electrician's helper. On the one hand, I hated my job because I could have gotten hurt by touching a live wire. On the other hand, I couldn't quit because I had no other way of earning a living. *In summary, I had the choice of hating my job or being out of work.*	I faced a *personal problem* when I worked as an electrician's helper. On the one hand, I hated my job because I could have gotten hurt by touching a live wire. On the other hand, I couldn't quit because I had no other way of earning a living. *In summary, dangerous jobs often pay well.*

Notice: The topic of both paragraphs is the problem the writer faced. The conclusion on the left-hand side summarizes what that problem is. The conclusion on the right-hand side has a different topic; it tells about dangerous jobs and how well they pay.

Chapter   8

Writing Introductions and Conclusions: Essays

Objective: to write an essay with a good introduction and conclusion

Vocabulary

Body— the middle part of a paragraph or essay

☞ Explanation:

The Introduction: The beginning, or first paragraph, of an essay is the introduction. When you are writing for tests such as the GED, your first paragraph should state your point of view, or what you think about the question.

The Body: The body of an essay is the paragraphs in the middle. These paragraphs give the important details.

The Conclusion: The conclusion is the last paragraph of the essay. Like the last sentence of the paragraph, it can summarize, solve a problem, or tell what will happen in the future.

PREVIEW

✏ EXERCISE A

Directions: The paragraphs in each essay below are not in the right order. Choose one of the two essays. Put "I" beside the introduction and "C" beside the conclusion. Put "1" and "2" beside the paragraphs that should go in between.

1. People often say, "The best things in life are free." Explain whether or not you agree with this saying; give good reasons for your opinion.

    a. _____ One important thing in life is your family. Yet, a family costs a lot of money. The head of a family must pay for the rent, food, and clothes. Also, both the parents and children need money to see movies, go bowling, or even have a little vacation.

    b. _____ People often say, "The best things in life are free." I do not agree with that saying.

    c. _____ Another important thing in life is your health. Doctors, dentists, and medicine all cost money. Even if you are not sick, you have to pay for checkups.

    d. _____ In conclusion, the best things in life are not free. People do not have to be rich, but they do need some money to be healthy and happy.

(*Check your answers, p. 142*).

2. A 1989 study showed that nearly 50% of inner-city teenagers do not finish high school. Why do you think so many teenagers choose not to finish? Give examples to explain what you mean.

    a. _____ If we cannot convince more teenagers to stay in school, our whole country will suffer. Many of these teenagers will not have jobs when they get older. Businesses will not be able to find people who can do the jobs that need to get done.

    b. _____ Second, the teenagers might have older friends who have quit school. When these friends brag about all the money they are earning, teenagers still in school often feel as though they should get a full-time job too. Even when students know that school will help them make more money over the years, they just may not want to wait.

    c. _____ Most teenagers have heard warnings not to drop out of school. Yet, many drop out anyway.

    d. _____ First, these teenagers are bored with school. School subjects do not seem to help them with their day-to-day problems. Subjects like history seem to talk about life as it used to be, not as it is today.

(*Check your answers, p. 142*).

EXERCISE B

Directions: Choose two of the four questions below. Write an essay for that question. Make sure you have a good introduction and conclusion. If you have completed an answer to question 1 or 2, compare it with the model on page 142.

Hint:

    a. To write a conclusion that summarizes, start with the words "in summary" or "to summarize."

    b. To write a conclusion that solves a problem, use the word "should" or "must."

    c. To write a conclusion that tells about the future, start with the word "if."

1. Are people doing enough to solve the problem of pollution? Explain your answer.

2. Some people say that "Two heads are better than one." Explain what this saying means by giving examples.

3. Many studies show that both children and adults often watch more than 4 hours of TV a day. Write an essay that explains why you think people watch so much TV.

4. According to a 1985 study, almost 10% of American adults cannot read. Write an essay that explains why our country has this problem.

_____

_____

_____

_____

_____

_____

_____

_____

_____

_____

_____

_____

_____

_____

Directions: Choose three of the paragraphs you wrote in the chapter that came before this one. Use the ideas in each paragraph to write an essay. Be sure to write a good conclusion for each essay. Write this in your writing notebook.

★ *Challenge Question:* The population of our country is getting older. More people today are "senior citizens" than ever before. Is this good or bad for our country? Explain your answer. Write this in your notebook.

✔ **Checklist:** Look over the essays you have written. Make sure that your conclusion fits the rest of the paragraphs in the essay.

Question: What is one problem many people face? Describe the problem and tell how it can be solved. Write this in your writing notebook.

Good conclusion

I faced a common problem when I had my first child.

I needed to keep on working, especially now that I had a baby to care for. On the other hand, I had no place to leave my baby. Besides, I really didn't want to leave her with babysitters all day.

Now, I have solved my problem. For my new job, I stay at home and call people on the telephone. This job has worked out well, because I can earn money and be with my daughter when she needs me.

To conclude, more mothers should try to find jobs they can do at home. Besides telephoning, they might be able to bake for a food store or type papers.

Poor conclusion

I faced a common problem when I had my first child.

I needed to keep on working, especially now that I had a baby to care for. On the other hand, I had no place to leave my baby. Besides, I really didn't want to leave her with babysitters all day.

Now, I have solved my problem. For my new job, I stay at home and call people on the telephone. This job has worked out well, because I can earn money and be with my daughter when she needs me.

To conclude, I still love my baby. In fact, I love her even more as she is starting to grow up. Having a child can be a problem, but it's worthwhile too.

Notice: The conclusion in the essay on the right-hand side tells how the writer feels about her baby; it does not tell about the problem.

Chapter 9

Correcting Your Sentences

Objective: to write a paragraph with correctly formed sentences

Vocabulary

> sentence fragment— sentence part, or incomplete sentence
> run-on— two sentences written as one
> revise— make your ideas better
> edit— correct writing mistakes

 Explanation: Did you ever wish you could take back what you said and start all over again? When you write a paragraph or essay, you get that chance. In fact, few people are satisfied with what they write the first time. Once they look over their work, they want to improve it.

The last step in the writing process is checking it over. When you check over your writing, you may revise it, by improving your ideas, or you may edit it by correcting any writing mistakes. In this chapter, you will practice correcting one common type of writing mistake: incorrectly written sentences.

Suppose someone said to you,

> "In the army."

You would wait for that person to say some more. The words "in the army" are only part of an idea. A complete sentence using these words might be,

> "My friend enlisted in the army."

Any group of words that starts with a capital letter and ends with a period should be a complete sentence. An incomplete sentence, or sentence fragment, looks like a complete sentence but is really only part of an idea.

Here are some rules for writing complete sentences.

a. Every sentence must have at least one subject and one verb.

Fragment: *For a good price.*

Sentence: *The dealer will sell me a car for a good price.*

Fragment: *Must take the night shift.*

Sentence: *New workers must take the night shift.*

Fragment: *People in the city.*

Sentence: *People in the city often live in crowded apartments.*

What are the subject and verb in each sentence?

b. Sentences with these words must either be a question or must have two subjects and two verbs:

who, where, what, when, how

Fragment: *who plays the guitar*

Sentence: *Who plays the guitar?*

Sentence: *Someone who plays the guitar will be at the party.*

What are the subjects and verbs in the sentences?

c. A sentence with these words must have more than one subject and verb:

whoever, wherever, whatever, whenever, however

Fragment: Whatever you say.
Sentence: We will do whatever you say.

What are the subjects and verbs in the sentence?

d. A sentence with these words must have more than one subject and verb.

if, unless, although, though, because

Fragment: If the restaurant is still open.
Sentence: If the restaurant is still open, I will get some pizza.

What are the subjects and verbs in the sentence?
(*Check your answers*, p. 142).

e. A sentence that starts with these words *may need* more than one subject and verb.

before, after, during, since, until, because

1. *Fragment:* Before the job interview.

Sentence a: I will find out about the company before the job interview.
Sentence b: I will find out about the company before the job interview starts.

2. *Fragment:* Because of the increase in taxes

Sentence c: The landlord raised my rent because of the increase in taxes.

Sentence d: The landlord raised my rent because taxes were increased.

What are the subjects and verbs in the sentences above?

(Check your answers, pp. 142–143).

PREVIEW

 EXERCISE A

Directions: Read the groups of words below. Write "S" if the words form a complete sentence. Write "F" if the words are a sentence fragment. Correct any sentence fragments by adding more words.

Hint: To complete a sentence fragment, think of when you have said these words yourself or heard someone else say them. What was the whole idea that you or the other person meant?

1. For one week.

_____

_____

2. There are too many cars in the city.

_____

_____

3. As soon as spring arrives.

_____

_____

4. The garage mechanic will know how to fix my car.

_____

_____

5. Although they knew how to do the job.

_____

_____

6. Which foods are most healthful.

_____

_____

(*Check your answers, p. 143*).

Task: Write a sentence that combines the ideas in a set of notes.

MODEL NOTES:

party, local union, goals — raise money, have fun, give to charity

Steps:

1. Say the words in each note to yourself.

2. Guess: What do these words mean?

3. Write this idea in a complete sentence.

4. Check the list of fragments above to be sure your sentence is complete.

MODEL SENTENCE: The local union is having a party to have fun and to raise funds for charity.

Notice: The sentence combined the ideas of <u>raising money</u> and <u>giving to charity</u>.

PREVIEW

 EXERCISE B

Directions: Choose two of the four sets of notes below. Write a sentence for that set of notes. Do not use the word "and" more than once.

1. Most Citizens

   may not agree with every action; government

   _____

   _____

2. Smart People

   may not know how to read and write well; can solve difficult problems

   _____

   _____

3. Television

   encourages you to read; makes you interested in places and people shown on the screen

   _____

   _____

4. City Air

   can cause breathing problems; fumes from cars and factories

   _____

   _____

(*Check your answers, p. 143*).

Run-on Sentences

Explanation: One common writing mistake is to make two sentences look like one.

Run-on: Many people live in mobile homes these homes can be towed from one place to another.

Run-on: Many people live in mobile homes, these homes can be towed from one place to another.

Sentence Pair: Many people live in mobile homes. These homes can be towed from one place to another.

Connected sentence: Many people live in mobile homes that can be towed from one place to another.

Task: Correct a run-on. Write either a sentence pair or a single sentence.

Steps:

1. Say each group of words slowly to yourself.
   Ask: Do I stop after any one of the words?

2. If you need to stop after a word, ask: Do the words on both sides form a complete sentence? If the answer is "yes," the sentence is a run-on.

   Run-on: Most mobile homes are sold already furnished (stop) the owner can move right in.

   Model sentence pair: Most mobile homes are sold already furnished. The owner can move right in.

   Model connected sentence: Most mobile homes are sold already furnished, so the owner can move right in.

PREVIEW

✏️ EXERCISE C

Direction: Write "S" if the words form two correct sentences. Write "R" if the words are "sentence run-ons." Correct the "run-ons."

1. Join the airforce, then learn to fly.

   _____

   _____

2. Because football can be dangerous, the players wear helmets.

   _____

   _____

3. I will watch TV, my favorite program is on.

   _____

   _____

4. No one said a word, everyone was waiting for the news program to begin.

   _____

   _____

5. I don't like my job, but I'm not planning to quit.

   _____

   _____

6. People who didn't vote should not complain about the election results.

   _____

   _____

(Check your answers, p. 143).

 EXERCISE D

Directions: Read the notes below. Write a sentence pair for two of the four sets of notes. Then connect your sentences into one. Do not use the word "and" more than once in each connected sentence. After you have completed your answer, compare it with the model on pages 143–144.

1. Firefighters
   work long hours
   often face danger
   save people

Sentence Pair: _____

_____

_____

Connected Sentence: _____

_____

_____

2. Computers

mathematical calculations
increasingly used
used at home and in office
do a variety of tasks
word processing

Sentence Pair: _____

_____

_____

Connected Sentence: _____

_____

_____

3. Different Problems

so many in our country
people can't decide which are most important
people can't decide which should be solved first

Sentence Pair: _____

_____

_____

Connected Sentence: _____

_____

_____

4. Writing Skills

are necessary
used to communicate with people who are far away
used to keep records of important events

Sentence Pair: _____

_____

_____

Connected Sentence: _____

_____

_____

Task: Correct the sentence fragments and run-ons in a paragraph.

Steps:

1. Read the whole paragraph.

> Watching fish swim in a fish tank helps people stay healthy. Many doctors keep fish in their offices. Because people find watching the fish relaxing. According to some studies. Watching fish in a tank prolongs people's lives, it reduces the number of strokes and heart attacks. Maybe more doctors should recommend fish tanks. To their patients.

2. Check the words up to the second period (after the word "offices"). Correct any sentence fragments and run-ons.

Watching fish swim in a fish tank helps people stay healthy. Many doctors keep fish in their offices, because people find watching the fish relaxing. According to some studies. watching fish in a tank prolongs people's lives, it reduces the number of strokes and heart attacks. Maybe more doctors should recommend fish tanks. To their patients.

3. Check the rest of the paragraph in the same way.

Watching fish swim in a fish tank helps people stay healthy. Since people find watching fish relaxing, many doctors keep fish in their offices. According to some studies, watching fish in a tank prolongs life, because it reduces the number of strokes and heart attacks. Maybe more doctors should recommend fish tanks to their patients.

EXERCISE E

Directions: The following paragraphs have correct sentences, sentence fragments, and run-ons. Edit one of the two paragraphs so that all the sentences are correctly formed.

1. *Question:* There is an old saying, "Blood is thicker than water." Explain what this saying means.

Paragraph: The saying "Blood is thicker than water" means that family ties are stronger. Than the ties of friends. People in a family have known each other, they are of the same 'blood,' they have lived in the same house since childhood. When sorrow strikes a person. Other members of that family feel almost as if they themselves have been struck.

2. *Question:* Many patriots show their love for their country by saying, "My country, right or wrong." Explain what this expression means and whether you agree with it.

    Paragraph: "My country, right or wrong," means that citizens should support their country. Even though it has many faults. For example, the United States has many problems, such as racism. And poverty. Just the same, it is still the best country in which to live. Citizens who love their country may feel sad about all its problems, they should work hard to correct what is wrong.

    (*Check your answers, p. 144*).

Directions: Write a paragraph that answers one of the three questions below. Be sure the sentences in your paragraph are correctly written. Write this in your writing notebook.

Remember: Brainstorm and organize your notes before you begin writing the paragraph.

1. Explain the meaning of the saying "Where there's a will there's a way." Give at least one example.

2. Think of famous person, such as a sports star, news announcer or actor. Do you think this person gets paid too much for what he or she does? Why or why not?

3. What are the advantages or disadvantages for participating in sports? Tell why you think the way you do.

Directions: Choose three paragraphs you wrote in the chapters before this one. Edit each paragraph, correcting any fragments and run-ons.

★ *Challenge Question:* Explain the meaning of the saying "No man is an island." Give at least one example. Check your paragraph for sentence fragments and run-ons. Write this in your writing notebook.

Chapter   10

Separating Your Paragraphs

Objective: to write essays with separate paragraphs

 Explanation: Another common writing mistake is to make your essay look like one, long paragraph. When you separate your paragraphs, you help the reader know when you are starting a new idea.

Task: Separate an essay into paragraphs.

Steps:

a. Read the whole essay quickly. Do not stop to read every word; just get the main idea.

Sample Question: Most people can remember times when they and their parents had trouble getting along. Give reasons why you think parents and children often argue, even though they may love each other. You may use your own experiences to think of good reasons.

MODEL ESSAY:

Most people can remember times when they did not get along with their parents, especially when they themselves were teen-agers. One reason for arguments between young people and their parents is that the young people are beginning to feel grown up. They are not ready to get a fulltime job, but they still feel old enough to take care of themselves. Certainly, they do not want advice from "the older generation." A second reason for family arguments may be the fault of parents who forget that their teenagers are not children any more. These parents may get upset when their son or daughter disagrees with them or want to do something the parents have never done before. In conclusion, both parents and teenagers have good reasons for their points of view. After all, parents' advice is worthwhile because it comes from experience. On the other hand, young people should make their own decisions about what is best for them.

b. Reread the beginning of the essay. Look for a change in the main idea while you are reading. Many times, clue words will help you find this change. The clue words may be:

1. "The first reason," "another reason"
2. "In conclusion," "to summarize"

c. Draw a slash just before the first sentence that changes the main idea. This is where the introduction ends and the body begins.

d. Read a little past the place where you have put the slash. Be sure that the main idea of the next sentence or two has really changed.

e. Read through the rest of the paragraph in the same way.

Most people can remember times when they did not get along with their parents, especially when they themselves were teen-agers. / One reason for arguments between young people and their parents is that the young people are beginning to feel grown up. They are not ready to get a fulltime job, but they still feel old enough to take care of themselves. Certainly, they do not want advice from "the older generation." / A second reason for family arguments may be the fault of parents who forget that their teenagers are not children any more. These parents may get upset when their son or daughter disagrees with them or want to do something the parents have never done before. / In conclusion, both parents and teenagers have good reasons for their points of view. After all, parents' advice is worthwhile because it comes from experience. On the other hand, young people should make their own decisions about what is best for them.

f. Rewrite the essay. Start a new paragraph with each slash. Reread the essay to be sure each paragraph starts in the right place. Write this in your writing notebook.

Most people can remember times when they did not get along with their parents, especially when they themselves were teenagers.

One reason for arguments between young people and their parents is that the young people are beginning to feel grown up. They are not ready to get a fulltime job, but they still feel old enough to take care of themselves. Certainly, they do not want advice from "the older generation."

A second reason for family arguments may be the fault of parents who forget that their teenagers are not children any more. These parents may get upset when their son or daughter disagree with them or want to do something the parents have never done before.

In conclusion, both parents and teenagers have good reasons for their points of view. After all, parents' advice is worthwhile because it comes from experience. On the other hand, young people should make their own decisions about what is best for them.

Notice: The first sentence is the introduction; it tells the main idea. Each paragraph in the body starts with a clue word such as "first" or "second." The conclusion starts with the words "in summary."

PREVIEW

  EXERCISE A

Directions: Rewrite the essay below, using separate paragraphs.

Question: Most people think that athletes have a wonderful job. Do you agree or disagree? Why?

Most people think that athletes have a wonderful job. Although being an athlete can be wonderful, it can cause problems, too. One problem many athletes have is a low salary. Most athletes do not make the big money that the stars do. Some athletes such as tennis and golf players even have to pay their own money to travel to different tournaments. If they don't win any prize money, they have less money than when they started! Athletes face a second problem when they grow older. Most athletes have to retire when they are still in their thirties, just as other people are beginning to get ahead. Jobs such as coaches or sports announcers are fun but hard for ordinary athletes to get. In conclusion, if you want to be an athlete, discuss the advantages and disadvantages with professionals already in the sport you are considering. Only then will you be ready to make the best decision for you.

_____

_____

_____

_____

_____

_____

_____

_____

_____

_____

_____

_____

_____

_____

✏️ EXERCISE B

Directions: The following essays have sentence fragments and run-ons. Also, they need to be divided into paragraphs. Rewrite one of the essays using correct sentences and separate paragraphs. After you have completed your answer compare it with the model on pp. 144–145.

Hint: First correct the sentence fragments and run-ons. Then separate the essay into paragraphs.

1. Think of one or two good friends you have. Define the word "friend" by explaining how you get along with this person.

    A friend is someone for whom you have a special feeling. And this friend has a special feeling for you in return. First, friends share their troubles. When you have a problem, a friend never laughs at you instead, the friend will help you figure out what to do. Friends are also important because they like to do the same things. You do. Watching sports on TV, fixing up old cars, or listening to rock music, almost anything you do is more fun. With a friend. These are just two examples of ways in which friends are important. Not everyone likes to do the same things that you like. Neither will everyone take the time. To help you solve a problem. That's why a friend is so special.

_____

_____

_____

_____

_____

_____

_____

_____

_____

_____

_____

_____

_____

2. Explain the meaning of the saying, "Pride goeth before a fall." Give examples.

People often say, "Pride goeth before a fall." This saying means that some people think they cannot make a mistake. In the end, they become careless, as a result, they fail. One example of a proud person headed for a fall is the boss who does not listen to the opinions of the other workers. In the end, such bosses may make mistakes, these mistakes could have been avoided had they talked to others. Another example that shows the truth of this saying is that of a football team after it has won a game. The players on the team might begin to think they are really great. Especially if their opponents have a good reputation. The players may decide they don't have to practice for the next game. In the end, the team may lose, simply because it was not prepared. In conclusion, to avoid a fall, people should listen to others, they should never be unprepared.

_____

_____

_____

_____

_____

_____

_____

_____

_____

_____

_____

_____

_____

Directions: Write an essay that answers one of the two questions below. Be sure your essay has correct sentences and separate paragraphs. Write this in your writing notebook.

1. Think of a problem that a particular group such as women, ethnic minorities, or the disabled have. Describe the problem and tell why it is important.

2. Our country spends billions of dollars every year to help poor and homeless people. Yet, studies show that many poor people and their children stay poor all their lives. Do you think Americans are doing enough to help the poor? Why or why not?

Directions: Choose three essays you have written from a previous chapter. Check your paragraphs to make sure that you have separated the paragraphs properly.

★ *Challenge Question:* Think of the important qualities a leader needs to have. Why are these qualities important for leaders such as the President of the United States, the president of a club, or the mayor of a town? Write this in your writing notebook.

Chapter   11

Revising and Editing: Paragraphs

Objective: to revise a paragraph or an essay

Vocabulary

    unified— belonging together

    clarify— make clear

    rough draft— first copy; paragraph or essay before it has been
                  revised or edited

    concise— not repetitious; said in as few words as possible

Explanation: In this chapter you will practice editing and revising your paragraphs and essays. When you edit, you will make sure your sentences and paragraphs are correctly formed. When you revise, you will polish your ideas and make sure they are well organized.

In some ways, then, this chapter is a review of all the chapters that came before it. You will be sure that all your ideas are:

    relevant—all your ideas help answer the question

    clearly stated—your first and last sentences clearly
    state your most important ideas

    organized—every idea is in the right place

    concise—you did not use extra words or repeat the same ideas

    correctly written—you have correctly formed sentences and paragraphs, with no spelling, grammar, or punctuation errors

When you are revising, remember:

YOU MUST BE PATIENT!

The process of revising is not hard; it just takes time. A good writer reviews his or her work *many* times!

Later on, you will get a chance to practice writing within a set period of time, just as you do for a test. For now, though, do not worry about the clock. Start getting into the habit of being *very, very careful.*

PREVIEW

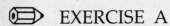 EXERCISE A

Directions: Revise one of the two paragraphs below so that it is relevant and clearly stated. Ask yourself these questions:

Relevant: Does my writing answer the question?

1. Is the main idea about the topic in the question?

2. Did you write what the "asking words" told you to write?

3. Does every sentence in the body have to do with the main idea?

4. Does the last sentence fit the rest of the sentences?

Clearly stated: Can the reader understand your main idea easily?

1. Does the introduction clearly state the main idea?

2. Does the conclusion clearly summarize the main idea or another important idea?

1. *Question:* A CT court once refused a 67-year-old woman the right to be a Boy Scout leader. Do you agree with the court's decision? After you have completed your answer, compare it with the model on p. 145.

    Rough draft:

    I think the court could have allowed the woman to be a Boy Scout leader. First, Boy Scouts should respect all people, whether they are male or female. Secondly, many young boys today don't have the chance to be around older people, since their grandparents often live in another city. In fact, the younger people may miss their grandparents as much as their grandparents miss them. By having an older woman as a leader, these boys might learn about other people. Thirdly, boys should learn that women as well as men can be good leaders. In summary, having a 67-year-old woman as leader could have happened to a Boy Scout troop but the court didn't let it.

Final copy:

_____

_____

_____

_____

_____

_____

_____

_____

_____

_____

_____

2. *Question:* Historians often claim that history repeats itself. Write a paragraph that explains what they mean and if you agree. Use specific examples to prove your point. After you have completed your answer, compare it with the model on p. 145.

Rough draft:

When historians say that history repeats itself they mean that they study the same things all the time. For example, stronger countries have attacked weaker countries in the past, just as they do in modern times. Also, many nations become powerful and then fall apart. This happened to Rome almost two thousand years ago and then it happened to the British Empire in this century. Of course, some historians don't agree that history really does repeat itself. In summary, history doesn't change.

Final copy:

_____

_____

_____

_____

_____

_____

_____

_____

_____

_____

_____

_____

✏️ EXERCISE B

Directions: Check the following paragraphs to be sure they are organized and concise. Ask yourself these questions:

Organized: Is every idea in the right place?

    1. Are the most important ideas first? Are the ideas in the order that they happened?
    2. Is each idea in the right sentence?

Concise: Are there any extra words or sentences?

    1. Does any sentence have extra words?
    2. Do any two sentences in the paragraph have the same meaning?

1. *Question:* Some people argue that wild animals should be left undisturbed in their natural habitat, rather than be captured and put in zoos. Give reasons explaining why you agree or disagree with this point of view. After you have completed your answer, compare it with the model on pp. 145–146.

Rough draft:

Wild animals should be left undisturbed in their natural habitat. They just don't belong in zoos. If all the animals are captured and put in zoos, scientists will not be able to study their natural behavior. Another reason is that keeping animals in zoos is unfair to the animals themselves. Many zoo animals are not as healthy as wild animals because zookeepers cannot feed them the foods found in woods and jungles. We may have no wild animals left if we capture too many animals for the zoos. Also animals in zoos and that are not wild are not happy because they cannot roam free. They cannot go where they want to go. These are the reasons why people should not try to capture animals and keep them cooped up in zoos.

Final copy:

_____

_____

_____

_____

_____

_____

_____

_____

_____

_____

_____

2. *Question:* Many people in our country are getting older. Therefore, more people today are senior citizens than ever before. Do you think this is good or bad for our country? Explain why. After you have completed your answer, compare it with the model on page 146.

Rough draft:

Our country is better because it has more senior citizens than ever before. First, because senior citizens often have extra time, they may be more willing to do volunteer work for free. In fact, many cities already use senior citizens and older people to tutor children in schools and cook meals for the homeless. Thus, many senior citizens are setting good examples for how to grow older and still remain useful. They work in libraries too.

Final copy:

_____

_____

_____

_____

_____

_____

_____

_____

_____

_____

_____

_____

EXERCISE C

Directions: Revise and edit one of the following paragraphs. Be sure it is relevant, clearly stated, organized, concise, and correctly written. After you have completed your answer, compare it with the model on p. 146. Write this in your writing notebook.

Remember: Check for sentence fragments and run-ons.

1. *Question:* Some people say, "For every cloud there is a silver lining." Write a paragraph that explains what this saying means and why you agree or disagree.

   "For every cloud there is a silver lining" means that every problem has a bright side. For example. People who lose their jobs often feel hopeless. Naturally, they are extremely unhappy and feeling sad; The chance to find a new and better job is like the silver lining in the cloud. Just the same, these people may really suffer if they don't find a good job soon. Another cloud that may that may have a silver lining is a failure in school. Or in business. Some studies have shown that the many successful people are those who have failed and learned from their mistakes. The lessons these people learned are the "silver lining" because they helped people succeed in the end.

2. *Question:* President Reagan once said that people who are hungry just don't know where to go. Do you agree with this statement? Write a paragraph that explains why or why not.

Rough draft:

President Reagan once said that people who are hungry just don't know where to go. Some people, especially those who live in rural areas, don't live near places that give out food, these people just live too far away. Other people are very old. And can't go to centers where food is being distributed. Other people, of course, would go if they knew of a place that had food. Also, many people are so sick. They can't get out of their houses to get the food. In summary, many people are still hungry in our country.

Directions: Choose three paragraphs you have written in the chapters before this one. Revise each paragraph so that the ideas are relevant, clearly stated, organized, concise, and correctly written. Write this in your writing notebook.

★ *Challenge Question:* Think about the things you would like to do to be successful. Explain what the word "success" means to you.

Chapter 12

Revising and Editing: Essays

Objective: to revise given and original essays

☞ **Explanation:** Revising and editing essays is like revising and editing paragraphs. Because essays are longer, though, you will spend a little more time improving your essays.

In this chapter, you will practice making sure your essay is:

Relevant: Does the essay answer the question?

    1.   Is the main idea about the topic in the question?
    2.   Does the main idea follow the directions in the "asking words" of the question?
    3.   Is every paragraph about the main idea of the whole essay?
    4.   Do all the sentences in each paragraph go together?
    5.   Does the conclusion fit the rest of the essay?

Clearly stated: Can the reader understand your main idea easily?

    1.   Does the introduction clearly state the main idea?
    2.   Does the last paragraph clearly summarize or draw a conclusion from the main idea?
    3.   Is the main idea in each paragraph clearly stated?

Organized: Is every idea in the right place?

    1.   Are the most important ideas first?
    2.   Is each idea in the right paragraph?

To the point: Are there any extra words or sentences?

    1. Does any sentence have extra words?

    2. Do any two sentences or paragraphs have the same meaning?

Correctly written: Are the sentences and paragraphs correctly formed?

    1. Is the essay free of sentence fragments and "run-ons"?

    2. Are the paragraphs separated in the right places?

PREVIEW

EXERCISE A

Directions: Each of the following questions has two rough drafts: one for an essay that answers "yes" and one for an essay that answers "no." Choose one question. Revise and edit both rough drafts for that question. After you have completed your answer, compare it with the model on pp. 146–147.

1. *Question:* We all know someone who has cheated in school. Many of us have cheated ourselves, at least once. Do you think a student who cheats on an important test should be expelled from school? Tell why you think the way you do.

Rough draft: YES

Too many people cheat! Whenever we have a test, at least one or two students pass answers to each other. Or take out papers they have copied from the book. This is a problem that occurs in all classes. No matter what the age of the students. Students who cheat on an important test are not interested in learning, they are interested only in getting a passing grade. Those students may be taking the place of other students who want to learn. Besides, if the school doesn't teach them to be honest now, they may learn the hard way—by getting fired from their job. Some students cheat by copying their papers from a book or magazine article. Those students might cheat once they get out of school and get a job. Also, if students who cheat are not expelled, everyone in the class suffers because the grades given for tests and papers are worthless. No one will know which students cheated and which students really earned their grades. In conclusion, allowing cheating harms both the cheater and the other students in the school. Therefore, cheaters should receive a harsh punishment for their actions.

Rough draft: NO

Students who cheat on an important test should be punished. However, they should not be expelled from school. First, some students might be cheating for the first time. These people should receive a harsh punishment only if they cheat again. For example, they can be made to take the test over again or be suspended for awhile. Then let them back into the school. Secondly, many students who cheat learn their lesson, they do not cheat again. Of course, not everyone who cheats gets caught and we really don't know how many times a person has cheated for sure. However, that is a problem we must ignore for now. A third reason for giving cheaters another chance is that they may be having trouble learning the material. The best way to help such people is to offer them special help. Either before or after classes. Fourth, those who want to expel cheaters from school should keep in mind what such a severe punishment might mean to the individual student. Students who are expelled may be so bitter they will never attend school again. Furthermore, they might lose their present job if their employer found out that they were dishonest and cheated. Therefore, expulsion from school should be used only when the student has cheated at least once and been warned of what the punishment will be. In summary, people who cheat should be given different punishments, depending on the circumstances.

2. *Question:* One of the most important laws in our society forbids stealing. Yet, sometimes people must steal food because they are hungry. Should these people be put in jail? Write an essay that tells what you think.

Rough draft: YES

People should be put in jail, no matter why they broke the law. People who steal food because they are hungry should be put in jail, just like other criminals. No one has to steal in order to get food to eat. Those who have no food stamps or money should try to get food from shelters or from churches set up for that purpose. If people knew they wouldn't be punished for stealing, they would steal even more than they do. When they were arrested, the thieves would just claim that they took food for survival. A judge would have a hard time proving that they were lying. Also, most poor people can get food stamps to use at the supermarket. In conclusion, hungry people who steal food are committing an unnecessary crime. That's just fair.

Rough draft: NO

People who steal when they are hungry should not be put in jail. First, these people probably would not steal if they had food to eat. They are just hungry and want to eat. Instead of spending the money to keep them in jail, society should give them food. Giving them food would help them out and prevent crime at the same time. This is a better solution because it is kinder and more helpful and more permanent. Second, people who steal food when they are hungry are not criminals. But they could become criminals if we put them in jail with others who steal even when they don't have to. They would learn how to pick locks and snatch purses from the criminals around them. Then our country would have more criminals, not less. Another problem made worse by putting people in jail when they steal from hunger is overcrowding in our jails. This problem is not caused by such actions but it is made worse by them. If we put such "criminals" in jail, we may have to let other, more violent criminals out on the streets. In conclusion, not all people steal because they are hungry. Those that do should not be made into criminals.

_____

_____

_____

_____

_____

_____

_____

_____

_____

_____

_____

_____

EXERCISE B

Directions: Choose one of the questions below. Write an essay that answers the question. Be sure to revise and edit your rough draft.

1. Today, almost one out of every ten members of America's armed forces is a woman. However, women have never been drafted in a war. Write an essay that tells whether you think this policy should be changed. Give reasons for your point of view. After you have completed your answer, compare it with the model on p. 148.

2. What are the advantages and disadvantages of being a man? Explain why you think the way you do.

3. What are the advantages and disadvantages of being a woman? Explain why you think the way you do.

_____

_____

_____

_____

_____

_____

_____

_____

_____

_____

_____

_____

_____

Writing

Directions: Choose three essays you have written in the chapters before this one. Revise and edit each essay so that the ideas are relevant, clearly stated, organized, to the point, and correctly written. Write this in your writing notebook.

★ *Challenge Question:* Some scientists argue that people's fates are determined from the time they are very young. Do you agree with this argument? Write an essay that explains why you agree or disagree with this argument. Be sure to revise and edit your "rough draft" and then write a final copy. Write this in your writing notebook.

Chapter 13

Freewriting

Objective: to freewrite paragraphs on topics of general interest

Vocabulary

point of view— one way of thinking about, or looking at, a topic

Explanation: Now that you have mastered the writing process, you are ready to tackle harder questions. These questions are more like those on writing tests such as the GED.

Many of the questions in the first part of this book were personal; these questions asked you to write about yourself. The second part of the book will have questions of wider interest, as well as personal ones. For example, a personal question might ask:

What is your favorite TV program? Why do you like it?

A question of wider interest might ask:

Do you think violence should be shown on TV? Why?

In order to answer the personal question, you must think of how a particular TV program affects only you. In order to answer the wider question, you must think of how violent programs affect different kinds of people. The questions in the second part of the book are more like those on tests such as the GED.

In this chapter, you will practice getting ideas about wider topics. This chapter is a warm-up for the second part of the book.

In order to write on a wide topic, you must step out of your own shoes and into the shoes of other people. Let's reread the question:

Do you think violence should be shown on TV? Why?

You yourself might like the excitement of a violent program every now and then. Yet, you must also think of other people who might watch the same program. How would the parents of a young child answer this question? What would a police officer who deals with criminals say? Would a teenager agree or disagree? What reasons would each give for his or her answer?

_____

_____

_____

_____

_____

_____

_____

_____

_____

_____

_____

_____

_____

_____

 EXERCISE A

Directions: Think of an argument or discussion you have had recently with someone. The argument could have been about an issue, or topic, that is discussed at work, in your town or city, or in the whole country. "Freewrite" a paragraph that gives your own point of view, or way of looking at the issue. Then "freewrite" a second paragraph that explains the other point of view. After you have completed your answer, compare it with the model on p. 148.

Hint: Think of everything you said on the topic, then "freewrite" your point of view. Remember that when you "freewrite," you do not have to worry about how good or bad your ideas are.

_____

_____

_____

_____

_____

_____

_____

_____

_____

_____

_____

_____

Now "freewrite" everything the other person said.

_____

_____

_____

_____

_____

_____

_____

_____

_____

_____

_____

_____

_____

_____

Task: "Freewrite" two paragraphs that answer a question. The first paragraph will answer "yes" and the second will answer "no."

Steps:

1. Draw a line down the center of your paper.

2. Think of all the ideas you can. Try to remember:

   a. conversations you have had with people you know. What did you say? Did the others agree with you? Why or why not?
   b. conversations you have heard on TV or radio "talk shows." How did the callers feel about the topic? What arguments did they use?
   c. news you learned from radio, TV, newspapers, or magazines. Did the reporters tell you how other people felt? Did the reporters tell you how they themselves felt?
   d. pictures or movie films from newspapers and TV. How did the pictures make you feel?

3. Write the "yes" ideas on the left side of the paper and the "no" ideas on the right side of the paper.

Sample Question: Every year, thousands of immigrants come to America from all over the world. Thousands more would come if they had the chance. Should the United States let more immigrants come here to work and live?

"Yes"
other people starving
only Indians didn't
come from another
country
we have enough jobs
and money to share

"No"
too many people want
to come
Americans lose jobs if
immigrants will take
less pay
immigrants have no
money
give to poor Americans,
not immigrants

4. Look over your ideas. Pick one point of view.

5. Use the notes on either the left or right side of the paper to express your point of view.

EXERCISE B

Directions: What do you think? Should the United States let more immigrants come here to work and live? Write a brief essay that answers the question. After you have completed your answer, compare it with the model on p. 149.

_____

_____

_____

_____

_____

_____

_____

_____

_____

_____

_____

Directions: Choose two of the four questions below. Write two paragraphs for each question. The first paragraph will give reasons why someone might agree with the statement and the second paragraph will give reasons why someone might disagree.

1. Should smoking be allowed in public places?

2. Should our country have higher taxes?

3. Is TV a good or bad force in our country?

4. Why are so many couples getting divorced nowadays?

_____

_____

_____

_____

_____

_____

_____

_____

_____

_____

_____

Chapter 14

Supporting with Details

Objective: to write an essay that uses details to support an opinion

Vocabulary

specific— telling about an exact time, place, person, or event
general— not specific or exact
detail— a specific piece of information; information about
an exact time, place, person, or event

 Explanation: Suppose you heard two people talking about crime in your city. Both think that the number of policemen should be increased. Which speaker is most likely to persuade you? Why?

Speaker A: The number of crimes in our city is increasing. Somehow, the city must stop this crime. In fact, some people signed a petition about the crime. These people claim that crime is causing them to lose money.

Speaker B: The number of violent crimes such as armed robbery and rape is increasing in our city. The city should have more policemen patrol places where the crime is taking place, particularly in large parking lots and in side streets. In fact, more than 100 merchants signed a petition asking the Mayor to have more police coverage in the evenings. These merchants claim that crime is costing them millions of dollars every year because shoppers are afraid to go out at night.

Speaker A's argument is too general. The argument presents the main idea, but it leaves out the details, or exact information.

The argument of Speaker B is more specific or exact. It uses

a. *Examples.* The speaker has given you two examples of the crimes being committed—armed robbery and rape.

b. *Details.* The speaker told you how the problem might be solved—by having more police coverage. It also includes specific information, that answers these questions:

> <u>what kind</u> of crimes (violent)
> <u>where</u> the crime is taking place (large parking lots, side streets)
> <u>who</u> signed the petition (more than a hundred merchants)
> <u>when</u> the police coverage should take place (in the evening)
> <u>how much</u> money the merchants claim they are losing (millions of dollars)

Can you find any other details this argument includes?

PREVIEW

 EXERCISE A

Directions: Read each of the sentence pairs below. Draw a line under the word or words that make the second sentence more specific than the first.

1. One major American city has no representatives in Congress because it is not part of a state or a territory.

   Washington, D.C. has no representatives in Congress because it is not part of a state or a territory.

2. One study estimated that many people live in a train station.

   A New York City study estimated that over 500 homeless people live in Grand Central station.

3. Some skills are becoming more and more needed.

   Skills such as word processing are becoming more and more needed in the job market.

4. Some jobs require their employees to work a certain number of hours a day.

   Most jobs require their employees to work seven or eight hours a day.

5. Many companies have insurance plans for their employees.

   Many companies have dental and medical insurance plans for all their employees.

(Check your answers, p. 149).

EXERCISE B

Directions: Choose four of the five sentences below. Revise the sentence so that it is more specific.

1. Some kinds of TV programs are more educational than other kinds.

_____

_____

_____

2. One or two people usually make the most important decisions in a family.

_____

_____

_____

3. If you cut yourself, put some medicine on the wound.

_____

_____

_____

4. Most TV commercials are short.

_____

_____

_____

5. Some problems of the city seem impossible to solve.

_____

_____

_____

(*Check your answers, p. 149*).

Task: Rewrite a paragraph to make it more specific.

Steps:

1. Write your details as notes at the side.

2. Use your notes to rewrite the sentences in the paragraph.

MODEL NOTES:

High school sports can be dangerous. Many players get hurt. Sometimes the injury lasts a long time. Some injuries are bad, too.	football, every year two dozen die knee operations

EXERCISE C

Directions: Use the model notes to rewrite the paragraph. After you have completed your answer, compare it with the model on p. 150.

_____

_____

_____

_____

_____

_____

_____

_____

_____

_____

_____

_____

_____

_____

PREVIEW

 EXERCISE D

Directions: Rewrite one of the two paragraphs below. Make them as specific as you can. Write this in your writing notebook. If you have completed an answer to question 1, compare it with the model on p. 150.

1. What is the worst problem the world faces today?

   War is the worst problem the world faces today. It has been going on for a long time. It hurts people and destroys whole villages in some countries. It does other bad things, too. Everyone wants to stop war, but no one knows what to do about it.

2. What is the worst problem America faces today?

   The worst problem America faces today is illiteracy. Illiterate adults have problems. The nation needs to find a solution to this problem.

 EXERCISE E

Directions: Choose one of the three questions below. Write a paragraph that answers the question you have chosen. Make your paragraph as specific as you can. Write this in your writing notebook. If you have completed an answer to question 1, compare it with the model on p. 150.

1. In 1989, the federal government passed a law prohibiting people from burning the American flag. Write a paragraph explaining whether or not you think people should be allowed to burn the flag. Give specific reasons or examples for your point of view.

2. Do you think our public schools are doing the best job they can to educate young people? Why or why not?

3. Probably you have heard people say, "Where there's a will there's a way." What does this expression mean?

Directions: Choose three paragraphs you have written before you started this chapter. Revise the paragraphs to make them more specific.

_____

_____

_____

_____

_____

_____

_____

_____

_____

_____

_____

_____

_____

_____

PREVIEW

 EXERCISE F

Directions: Revise one of the two essays below by making it more specific. Write this in your writing notebook. If you have completed an answer to question 1, compare it with the model on p. 150.

Hint: Write your details as notes at the side. To keep track of which notes you have used, check off each set of notes as you write.

1. What are the most important problems big cities have?

    Essay:

    Big American cities have many problems.

    First, the cities have many poor people. The city governments try to help these people, but the number of people who cannot afford anything is getting bigger.

    Second, the cities are getting too crowded. This causes a lot of other problems.

    Third, the pollution in the cities is getting worse. There are many causes for this problem and the city governments should do something about it.

If the cities can't solve their problems soon, people won't want to live there any more.

2. Throughout the years, America has been called "the land of golden opportunity." Why has it been given this name? Do you think it really is a land of "golden opportunity? Why or why not?

Essay:

America has been called by others "the land of golden opportunity" because it offers the chance to become rich. However, I don't think America really offers a golden opportunity to most people.

First, many Americans have suffered because of prejudice. Many Americans aren't given an equal chance because of the color of their skin or because of other things.

Second, many Americans who are born poor stay poor all their lives. People who are born rich stay rich all their lives. There are a lot of reasons for this.

In conclusion, many people who don't live in America don't have a true picture of our country.

✐ EXERCISE G

Directions: Write an essay for one of the following two questions. Write this in your writing notebook. If you have completed an answer to question 1, compare it with the model on pp. 150–151.

1. Explain how your life would change if you won a million dollars. In what ways would your life stay the same?

2. One of the biggest changes in life is the role of women as wives and mothers in the home and as workers in the marketplace. Explain what you think should be the ideal role of women as family members and as workers.

Directions: Choose three essays you have written before you started this chapter. Revise the essays to make them more specific. Write this in your writing notebook.

★ *Challenge Question:* One popular saying is, "People are their own worst enemies." Write an essay that explains what this saying means and whether or not you agree with it. Give specific reasons and examples for your point of view. Write this in your writing notebook.

Chapter 15

Explaining Why

Objective: to use reasons to support an opinion

Vocabulary

> fact— information that can be proven
> logical— making sense
> informative— giving information

 Explanation: When you want to present your point of view, you must tell *why* you think the way you do. Your reasons will be convincing only if they are informative, complete, and logical.

Informative reasons: Each sentence below should tell the reader *why* water should not be polluted. Which sentence is more convincing?

> *Sentence A:* People should not pollute the water because pollution is bad.

> *Sentence B:* People should not pollute the water because pollution makes water unsafe to drink.

Hint: Which sentence repeats an opinion? Which sentence adds more information? Write this in your writing notebook.

PREVIEW

 EXERCISE A

Directions: Read the sentence pairs below. Only one of the sentences in each pair adds information. Put a check beside that sentence.

1. a. Husbands should help their wives clean the house because their wives deserve it.

   b. Husbands should help their wives clean the house because both husbands and wives live in it.

2. a. Our school needs more classes because it does not have enough of them.

   b. Our school needs more classes because there is a long waiting list to get into every class.

3. a. People should be fined for littering because picking up litter costs the city money.

   b. People should be fined for littering because littering is wrong.

4. a. People should not pollute the water because pollution is dirty.

   b. People should not pollute the water because pollution makes the water unsafe to drink.

5. a. The parking lot is full because so many people came to see the parade.

   b. The parking lot is full because there are no empty spaces.

   (*Check your answers, p. 151*).

 Explanation: *Complete reasons:* Suppose you read one of the following statements in the newspaper? Which statement would convince you more? Why? Write this in your writing notebook.

   Statement A: The city workers may strike because their contract is expiring.

   Statement B: The city workers may strike because they can't agree with the Mayor on a new contract.

Hint: Do workers always strike every time their contract expires? Which statement best explains why the city workers may strike? Write this in your writing notebook.

PREVIEW

 EXERCISE B

Directions: Read the sentence pairs below. Only one of the sentences in each pair is complete. Put a check beside that sentence.

Hint: Which sentence does not make the reader guess what the author is thinking?

1. a. The battery wore out because the radio had been on for over eight hours.

   b. The battery wore out because the radio had been on.

2. a. The citizen was suspected of being a traitor because he had state secrets.

   b. The citizen was suspected of being a traitor because he was caught passing state secrets to a spy for an enemy country.

3. a. A minimum wage law affects younger workers more than older ones because younger workers usually are less experienced.

   b. A minimum wage law affects younger workers more than older ones because younger workers usually are less experienced and have lower salaries.

4. a. The city needs to raise taxes because the lack of services is causing many people to leave.

   b. The city needs to raise taxes because many people are leaving.

5. a. People should wear seat belts because there are so many automobile accidents.

   b. People should wear seat belts because seat belts help people survive automobile accidents.

   (*Check your answers, p. 151*).

 Explanation: *Logical reasons:* Suppose you heard the following statements on TV? Which statement would make the most sense to you? Why?

   Statement A: Most people didn't care who won the election because they didn't vote.

   Statement B: Most people didn't vote because they didn't care who won the election.

Hint: Which came first in real life the fact that people didn't care or the fact that they didn't vote?

PREVIEW

 EXERCISE C

Directions: Read the sentence pairs below. Put a check beside the sentence in each pair that is logical, or that makes sense.

Hint: The real cause should follow a word such as *because*, *if*, or *since*.

1. a. The parents were disturbed over their child's behavior because they couldn't sleep at night.

   b. The parents couldn't sleep at night because they were disturbed over their child's behavior.

2. a. Since many adults lack a high-school diploma, they are going back to school.

   b. Since many adults are going back to school, they lack a high-school diploma.

3. a. The bill will become a law because the President signed it.

   b. The President signed the bill because it will become a law.

4. a. People are frustrated about prejudice and poverty because they riot.

   b. People riot because they are frustrated about prejudice and poverty.

5. a. America is the "land of opportunity" because many people come here.

   b. Many people come to America because it is the "land of opportunity."

   (*Check your answers, p. 151*).

Task: Complete each sentence by writing a reason.

Steps:

1. Read the first part of the sentence.

   The government should have health insurance because

2. Think of a fact that gives more information; be sure the fact tells *why* the first part of the sentence is true.

The government should have health insurance because many sick people can't afford to go to the doctor.

3. Check your reason to be sure it

    a. does not reword the opinion stated in the first part of the sentence.

    b. gives all the information needed.

    c. makes sense.

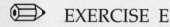 EXERCISE D

Directions: Complete three of the four sentences below. Write a convincing reason in each blank.

Remember: You do not have to agree with the sentence to write a real reason.

  1. Having basic math skills is important because _____

      _____

  2. Computers are becoming more popular because _____

      _____

  3. People should save as much as they can because _____

      _____

  4. A strong national army is important because _____

      _____

(*Check your answers, p. 151*).

PREVIEW

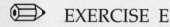 EXERCISE E

Directions: Each question below has two answers—each with a different point of view. Choose two of the three questions. Then choose the point of view you find easiest to support for each of these questions. Revise the paragraph so that it is more convincing. If you have completed an answer to question 1, compare it with the model on p. 151.

Hint: Cross out any sentences in the body of the paragraph that do not give convincing reasons for the main idea. Add more good reasons if you can.

1. *Question:* Do you think people should use credit cards? Why or why not?

    a. *People should use credit cards.* Credit cards are safer to carry around than money, because the card owner can always report a stolen card. Also, credit cards are necessary and most people can't do without them. Stores like them too.

    b. *People should not use credit cards.* Many people use credit cards because they run out of money. However, they may charge so many bills that they can't pay later on. Then it's too late. The damage is done. Also, using credit cards raises prices because stores pay credit card companies a percentage of every purchase made with their cards. Credit cards aren't good for the people who buy or the people who sell.

    _____

    _____

    _____

    _____

    _____

    _____

    _____

2. *Question:* Many states have laws requiring people to wear seat belts. Do you agree with these laws? Why or why not?

    a. *The law should not make people wear seat belts* because it's a free country. Furthermore, some women may be pregnant or overweight because they can't wear seat belts. Seat belts may not be safe or comfortable for these people. In conclusion, people who do not want to wear seat belts should be able to do as they please.

    b. *The law should make people wear seat belts.* Studies done in the last five years show that many people don't wear seat belts. Also, many people don't want to wear seat belts. Making everyone wear a seat belt would save lives.

    _____

    _____

_____

_____

_____

_____

_____

_____

3. *Question:* When most companies lay off some workers, they lay off the ones who were hired most recently. Is this policy fair? Why or why not?

    a. *Companies should lay off the workers who were last hired.* Most of these workers are younger than the ones who have been there a long time. They can't do the job as well. Also, they probably don't need the money as much as the older workers.

    b. *Companies should keep the best workers and fire the others.* The best workers probably have many family responsibilities because they work harder and get paid more. Also, any other policy would be unfair.

_____

_____

_____

_____

_____

_____

_____

Task: Write a paragraph that tells *why.*

Steps:

1. Fold your paper in half. Brainstorm all the reasons why you agree on one side of the paper and all the reasons why you disagree on the other.

2. Choose the side you can support the best.

3. Use your ideas to write the paragraph.

4. Check to be sure your reasons are informative, complete, and logical.

EXERCISE F

Directions: Choose three of the five questions below. Write a paragraph that answers the question in each paragraph. Give good reasons for your answers. If you have completed an answer to question 1, compare it to the model on pp. 151–152.

1. The majority of people in jail are poor. Yet, many people argue that our justice system is fair to the poor as well as to the rich. Do you agree with this statement? Explain why you agree or disagree.

_____

_____

_____

_____

_____

_____

_____

_____

_____

2. Studies show that many workers prefer companies that provide free day care service for their young children. Do you think more businesses should have day care centers? Give reasons for your opinion.

_____

_____

_____

_____

_____

_____

_____

_____

3. Some people claim that we get wiser as we get older. Do you agree? Explain why or why not.

    _____

    _____

    _____

    _____

    _____

    _____

    _____

4. By law, all workers in a trade do not have to belong to a union. Do you think all workers should join a union, even though it is not required by law? Support your answer.

    _____

    _____

    _____

    _____

    _____

    _____

    _____

5. As the average age of Americans gets older, more and more workers are reaching the age when they can retire. Should senior citizens be allowed to continue working as long as they want or should they be forced to retire after a certain age? Why do you feel the way you do?

    _____

    _____

    _____

_____

_____

_____

_____

_____

Task: Write an essay that tells *why*.

Follow the same steps as you did when writing a paragraph. Remember:

1. Brainstorm your ideas that agree and disagree on each side of the folded paper.

2. Choose the side with the best reasons and write your essay.

3. Check to be sure your reasons are informative, complete, and logical.

EXERCISE G

Directions: Choose two of the four questions below. Write an essay that answers each question. Be sure to give good reasons for your answer. Write this in your writing notebook. If you have completed an answer to question 1, compare it with the model on p. 152.

Hint: Start a new paragraph for each reason.

1. Every time a country goes to war, some citizens refuse to fight because they think the war is wrong. Should these people be put in jail? Write an essay that tells what you think and why you think the way you do.

2. Many people claim that gun control laws would reduce the number of crimes committed in this country. Should our country have stricter regulations for carrying a gun? Why or why not?

3. Think of one job that is underpaid. Explain why you think the people who do that job should get more money.

4. In most of our major cities, homeless people are lying in the street or begging for money, even though the cities have shelters for them. Should all homeless people be forced to get off the streets and go into shelters? Give reasons for your opinion.

★ *Challenge Question:* Write two essays that answer the question below. The first essay will tell why someone might agree with the statement. The second essay will tell why someone might disagree. Write this in your writing notebook.

   After World War II, most historians agreed that the United States was the leader of the "free world." What do you think this statement means. Give reasons why you think this statement is still true or not true.

Chapter 16

Comparing and Contrasting

Objective: to write essays that compare and contrast

Vocabulary

compare— tell how two ideas are alike
contrast— tell how two ideas are different

☞ **Explanation:** Some test questions may ask you to compare or contrast. To compare is to tell how two ideas are alike; to contrast is to tell how two ideas are different. Certain "clue words" may help you compare or contrast.

Compare: _Just as_ individuals are forced to obey the laws of their country, _so_ the different nations should be forced to obey the laws of an international organization.

Contrast: People used to wait weeks for mail from a different country, _but_ today we can fax messages and documents in a few moments.

What two ideas do the clue words "just as" compare? What two ideas does the clue word "but" contrast? Write this in your writing notebook.

PREVIEW

 EXERCISE A

Directions: Underline the two ideas contrasted in the paragraph below. Then circle the clue words.

> The jobs of a supermarket bagger and a mailcarrier are very different. Whereas a bagger works inside the store, a mail carrier usually stays outdoors. Another difference is that, unlike a mail carrier, a bagger may have to work in the nighttime or on Sundays when the store is open. In summary, a supermarket bagger's workplace and hours are different from those of a mail carrier.

(Check your answer, pp. 152–153).

 EXERCISE B

Directions: Choose one of the two questions below. Write a paragraph that answers the question. If you have completed an answer to question 1 compare it with the model on p. 153.

Hint: Contrast with clue words such as *unlike, whereas, but, although, however, on the other hand, in contrast.*

1. In what ways is life today different from life as it was when your parents were young?

2. Think back on the hobbies, type of work, likes and dislikes of your mother or father. Write a brief paragraph explaining the ways in which you are different from her or him.

_____

_____

_____

_____

_____

_____

_____

PREVIEW

EXERCISE C

Directions: Underline the two ideas compared in the paragraph below. Then circle the clue words.

The jobs of a supermarket bagger and a mailcarrier are alike in many ways. The bagger often has to lift and carry heavy bags of groceries. Similarly, a mailcarrier has to carry heavy bags of mail. Also, both a bagger and a mailcarrier wear uniforms.

(*Check your answers, p. 153*).

EXERCISE D

Directions: Choose one of the three questions below. Write a paragraph that answers the question. If you have completed an answer to question 1 or 2, compare it with the models on p. 153.

Hint: Compare with clue words such as *just as, similarly, in the same way, like, both.*

1. Think back on the hobbies, career plans, likes and dislikes that you had ten years ago. Write a brief paragraph explaining the ways in which you are the same as you were then.

_____

_____

_____

_____

_____

_____

_____

2. In what ways is life today the same as life when your parents were young?

_____

_____

_____

_____

_____

_____

_____

_____

3. Think of the hobbies, type of work, likes and dislikes of your mother or father. Explain the ways in which you are like this parent.

_____

_____

_____

_____

_____

_____

_____

_____

PREVIEW

✏️ **EXERCISE E**

Directions: Circle the clue words used to compare in the paragraph below. Then circle the clue words used to contrast.

> The jobs of a supermarket bagger and a mailcarrier are both alike and different. The bagger often lifts and carries heavy bags of groceries. In the same way, the mailcarrier often lifts and carries heavy bags. On the other hand, the supermarket bagger often has to work in the late evenings and on Sundays, whereas the mailcarrier does not.

(*Check your answers, p. 153*).

Task: Write a paragraph that both compares and contrasts.

Steps:

1. Draw a line that divides your paper in half. Put the word "alike" at the top of the column on the left side of your paper and the word "different" at the top of the column on the right.

2. Brainstorm your ideas. Put a note for each idea in the column where it belongs.

3. Decide if you will compare or contrast. Use the clue words to compare or contrast when you write.

4. Check over your ideas to be sure they are clear.

EXERCISE F

Directions: Choose two of the three questions below. Write a paragraph that answers the question by both comparing and contrasting. Write this in your writing notebook. If you have completed an answer to question 1, compare it with the model on p. 153.

1. If you were the manager of your workplace, how would you keep things the same and how would you make them different? Compare and contrast your own ideas with those of your manager.

_____

_____

_____

_____

_____

_____

_____

_____

2. Think about the school you attended and the school you attend now. In what ways should our educational system be changed? In what ways should it be kept the same?

_____

_____

_____

_____

_____

_____

_____

_____

3. In what ways are people's lives the same all over the world? In what ways are they different?

_____

_____

_____

_____

_____

_____

_____

_____

Task: Write an essay that compares and contrasts. Follow the same steps as you did when writing a paragraph.

Remember:

1. Fold your paper in half. Label one side "same" and the other side "different."

2. Brainstorm your ideas and put them in the "same" and "different" columns.

3. Use the clue words to compare and contrast as you write your essay.

4. Check over your essay to be sure your ideas are clear.

✏️ EXERCISE G

Directions: Choose two of the four questions below. Write an essay that compares and contrasts for each question. Write this in your writing notebook. If you have completed the answer to question 1, compare it with the model on p. 154.

Hint: Use separate paragraphs for the ideas that compare and contrast.

1. In what ways is the role of women the same today as it was 40 years ago? In what way is it different?

2. In what ways do you think our country will change over the next 40 years? In what ways do you think it will remain the same?

3. In what ways are men and women alike? In what ways are they different?

4. If you were the mayor of your city, what changes would you make? What policies would you keep the same?

★ *Challenge Question:* Write an essay that explains the similarities and differences between a democracy and a dictatorship. Write this in your writing notebook.

Chapter 17

Refuting the Opposite Point of View

Objective: to state and refute the opposite point of view

Vocabulary

refute— give reasons why you disagree with the opposite point of view

Explanation: Suppose you live alone and your widowed mother wants to move in. You do not think this is a good idea, but you don't want to hurt her feelings, either. Here is one argument you might use to convince her.

I know that you want to live with me. Yet, I don't think you would be happy if you did.

Although you are lonely living alone, moving into my apartment might make the problem worse. First of all, I'm not home most of the time, since I work during the day and go to school at night. Second, although most of your friends have moved away, you still have a few left near your own home.

Another reason why you might be unhappy is that we will be crowded. You said you would be willing to sleep on the couch in the living room. However, I would keep you up any time I watched TV late at night or had friends over for the evening.

In summary, living with me would make you feel more lonely and unhappy than you are now.

Now reread the argument above, paying special attention to the underlined words. These are your mother's reasons for wanting to live with you. Notice that the essay tells why you disagree with each reason. When you tell why you disagree, you are refuting the opposite point of view.

The arguments stating the opposite point of view are on the left side and the arguments that refute the opposite point of view are on the right.

Opposite point of view (*mother's*)	Refuting arguments (*writer's*)
You are lonely.	Moving into the apartment might make the problem worse.
Most of your friends have moved away.	You still have a few friends near your own home.
You can sleep on the couch in the living room.	I would keep you up when I watch TV late at night or have friends over for the evening.

Task: Identify the ideas that state the opposite point of view.

Steps:

1. Underline the main idea of the paragraph in the first and last sentences.

2. Reread the rest of the paragraph. Put a check above each sentence or sentence part that agrees with the main idea.

Sample Question: Some studies show that more than half of the women in America go to work while their children are still young. Should businesses help working parents by providing free day care for their employees? Write a paragraph that tells what you think and why.

Businesses should provide free day care for the children of their workers. Although this day care may be expensive, it will save the businesses money, because parents will not have to stay home every time the babysitter doesn't come Workers without young children may claim that the benefit of free day care is unfair because it is a benefit that they don't need; however, this benefit is just as fair as "sick days," which some workers may need and others may not.

3. Reread each sentence or sentence part that is left. Circle the sentence or sentence part if it gives the opposite point of view.

Businesses should provide free day care for the children of their workers. Although this day care, may be expensive, it will save the businesses money, because parents will not have to stay home every time the babysitter doesn't come. Workers without young children may claim that the benefit of free day care is unfair because it is a benefit that they don't need; however, this benefit is just as fair as "sick days," which some workers may need and others may not.

Notice: Arguments that give the opposite point of view come before the arguments that refute.

PREVIEW

 EXERCISE A

Directions: Read each question below. Then read the two paragraphs underneath. One paragraph answers the question "yes" and the other answers the question "no."

Choose either the "yes" or the "no" paragraph. Draw a line under the main idea, then draw a circle around each sentence or sentence part that states the opposite point of view.

> *Question:* A 1989 poll showed that most Americans think that drug abuse is our country's worst problem. Do you think the best way to solve this problem is by putting everyone who abuses or sells drugs in jail? Why or why not?

> *Paragraph:* YES
> Some people say that educating young people about the dangers of drugs is the best way to reduce drug abuse. Although education has a more lasting effect than any other solution, it will not solve the immediate problem of getting drug dealers off the streets. Nor will it persuade those who are already addicts to quit their habit. In contrast, if everyone who abused or sold drugs were put in jail, the rest of the people might be afraid to get involved too.

> *Paragraph:* NO
> Many people think the government could reduce the use of illegal drugs by putting more drug abusers and dealers in jail. However, if every abuser or dealer were jailed, our prisons would be so overcrowded that we would have to let some criminals go free. Therefore, we should spend the money to educate young people about the dangers of drugs. Although this solution would take more time, it would have a lasting effect. Illegal drugs would simply disappear from our streets because no one would want them any more.

> (*Check your answers, p. 154*).

 EXERCISE B

Directions: Choose two of the three questions below. Write a paragraph that answers each question. Be sure to refute the opposite point of view in each paragraph. If you have completed an answer to question 1, compare it with the model on p. 155.

1. One common saying is, "Cream rises to the top." This saying means that those who deserve success get it in the end. Do you agree with this saying? Why or why not?

_____

_____

_____

_____

_____

_____

_____

_____

_____

_____

_____

_____

_____

2. Many people today claim that our country is becoming separated into two societies—one "black" and one "white." Do you agree with this claim? Why or why not?

_____

_____

_____

_____

_____

_____

_____

_____

_____

_____

_____

_____

_____

_____

3. As more and more immigrants come to the United States, the number of people who do not speak English is growing. Should people who cannot speak or understand English be allowed to vote?

_____

_____

_____

_____

_____

_____

_____

_____

_____

_____

_____

Task: Identify the opposite point of view and the arguments used to refute it in an essay.

Steps:

1. Underline the main idea in the introduction.

2. Underline the main idea in each paragraph of the body.

3. Circle the opposite point of view.

4. Underline the main idea in the conclusion.

Notice: Which comes first—the main idea or the opposite point of view?

PREVIEW

EXERCISE C

Directions: Read the question below. Then read the two essays underneath. One essay expresses a "yes" point of view and the other expresses a "no" point of view.

Choose one essay. Draw a line under the main idea in the paragraph. Then draw a circle around the sentence or sentence part that states the opposite point of view in each paragraph of the essay. After you have completed your essay, compare it with the model on p. 155.

Question: More and more women are going back to work within a few months of having a baby. Do you think they should stay home and take care of their babies?

Essay: YES

All women with babies should go back to work if they want to. Women should have the same rights to work or to stay at home as men do.

Some people argue that mothers of young children should work only if they need the money. Yet, each family should be able to decide for itself what is "enough money."

Other people argue that children with mothers at home are happier than the children of working mothers. However, caring for a child at home does not guarantee that the child will be better adjusted. In fact, many children whose mothers stay at home do not grow up to be well-adjusted.

In conclusion, every mother should decide for herself what is best for her and her children.

Essay: NO

All women with babies should not go back to work. They should stay at home and care for their babies for at least a few years.

Some people argue that some mothers cannot afford to stay at home while their babies are young. However, the well-being of a woman's family is more important than any money she could earn.

Other people argue that each mother should decide for herself what is best for her and her family. This argument ignores the fact that all babies have the same need: one person who can care for them when they are sick and play with them when they are well. No one can do that job as well as a mother can.

In summary, caring for a baby is a fulltime job. Therefore, all mothers should not work outside the home until their babies are older.

Task: Use notes to write an essay that refutes the opposite point of view.

Steps:

1. Draw a line from the notes that give one point of view to the notes that refute that point of view.

2. Choose a "yes" or "no" point of view.

3. Write an introduction that states your main idea.

4. Use the notes to state your point of view and to refute the opposite point of view.

5. Write a conclusion.

EXERCISE D

Directions: Read the question below. Use the notes to write an essay that answers "yes" or "no." Be sure to refute the opposite point of view. Write this in your writing notebook. After you have completed your answer, compare it with the model on pp. 155–156.

Hint: Put opposite point of view first.

Question: Capital punishment is the practice of killing people for crimes they have committed. In this country, criminals are not executed unless their crimes involved the loss of life. Do you think capital punishment is fair? Why or why not?

Notes:

Yes	No
a. saves money	a. wrong people can be executed
b. poor as well as rich murderers may be executed	b. cost of getting sentence changed
c. prevents others from committing murder	c. states without capital punishment don't have lower murder rate
d. murderers can't escape	d. unfair because most people executed are poor
e. only used in cases where judge and jury are sure	

Essay

_____

_____

_____

_____

_____

_____

_____

_____

_____

_____

_____

_____

_____

✏️ EXERCISE E

Directions: Choose two of the four questions below. Write an essay that answers the question you have chosen. Be sure your essay refutes the opposite point of view. If you have completed an answer to question 1 or 2, compare it with the model on p. 156.

1. In 1987, the National Collegiate Athletic Association said that high school athletes should have a certain grade point average and SAT score in order to be accepted into college. Write an essay that explains whether or not high school athletes should be admitted to college, even if they have low grades or a low SAT score.

2. In 1989, the State of Oregon passed a law saying that people over 80 could not receive medicaid for services such as major surgery. Do you think such a law is fair? Explain why or why not.

3. Everyone has had the experience of eating in a favorite restaurant, only to have the meal spoiled by a crying child. Write a paragraph that tells whether or not you think little children should be allowed in fancy restaurants. Give reasons why you think the way you do.

4. Should high school students be paid as much as older workers for doing the same jobs? Give reasons for your point of view.

_____

_____

_____

_____

_____

_____

_____

_____

_____

_____

_____

_____

_____

_____

Directions: Choose three essays you wrote before you started this chapter. Rewrite the essay so that it also refutes the opposite point of view. Write this in your writing notebook.

★ *Challenge Question:* Write an essay explaining whether or not you think people are too materialistic, or too concerned about cars, beautiful homes, clothes, and other goods that money can buy. Write this in your writing notebook.

Chapter 18

Timing Yourself

When you are taking the GED, you will have about 45 minutes to complete a 200-word essay. This chapter will give you practice timing yourself while you are writing. You need this practice if:

- you finish your essays more than five minutes early.

- you do not have time for ALL the writing steps, including editing and revising.

The 10-25-10 Plan: The 10-25-10 plan is one way of keeping track of the minutes as you are working. According to this plan, you should spend:

a. 10 minutes on the first two steps on the plan—thinking about the question and brainstorming your ideas.

b. 25 minutes putting your ideas on paper.

c. 10 minutes revising and editing.

The 10-25-10 plan is not exact. After you have practiced writing timed essays, you may decide on a plan of your own. Be sure, though, that you are not taking less than 7 or 8 minutes on brainstorming or less than 5 minutes on revising and editing.

FINISHING TOO EARLY: If you are finishing more than 7 or 8 minutes early, you are cheating yourself by not taking the time to write your very best essay.

First, decide which stage of the writing process is being done too quickly. Look over your writing and ask:

Am I making sure my essay really answers the question?

Am I brainstorming enough ideas? Do I look over these ideas to be sure they are relevant? Am I organizing my ideas before I start my essay?

Am I writing good introductions? Do my conclusions fit the rest of the essay?

Am I correcting any mistakes after I am finished?

Some students rush through every step of the writing process. Others rush through some steps and take their time on the rest; the two steps that students most often do hastily are the preplanning and editing stages.

Rushing through one or more steps of the writing process is a hard habit to break. In fact, you may not be able to break it all at once. Keep timing yourself as you write, making sure that you are following the 10-25-10 plan.

When you are finished, jot down the number of minutes you took. Try to make yourself take a little longer each time. Compare the essay you have just finished with the ones you did in a shorter time. Did taking more time improve your writing? In what way?

FINISHING TOO LATE: You are finishing too late if part of your essay is still unwritten or if you do not have the time to revise and edit your work at the end.

Time yourself according to the 10-25-10 plan and see which stage is taking too long. Are you worrying too much about each word or idea? Is your mind wandering so that you are spending minutes daydreaming when you should be writing?

Like rushing through the essay, taking too much time is a hard habit to break. Practice writing while glancing at you watch regularly. Go just a little faster each time, telling yourself that you will be able to revise or edit at the end.

PRACTICING TIMED ESSAYS: In order to be ready for the test, you might want to practice timed essays ahead of time. Follow these rules while you are practicing:

- Find a quiet place to work. Perhaps you are so used to noise that it does not bother you. However, you should get used to working in a quiet room just like the one in which you will take the test.

- Write in one block of time, without any interruptions. When you take the GED, you will write for 45 minutes, no matter how tired or restless you feel. Therefore, when you are practicing, do not stop to answer the phone or have a snack. Think of your writing session as a form of exercise. Just as you must exercise in order to jog or swim without getting out of breath, you must practice writing without letting your mind wander.

–Time yourself as you write. If you do not time yourself while you are practicing, the chances are good that you will work too fast or too slow on the test itself.

Directions: Write a 200-word essay for each of the questions below. Time yourself so that you do not take more than 45 minutes. Do each essay at a separate time.

TIMED QUESTIONS:

1. Do you think Americans should buy only American-made cars? Why or why not?

_____

_____

_____

_____

_____

_____

_____

_____

_____

_____

_____

_____

2. Right now, you are working to get an "education." Explain what you think makes a person educated. How is an educated person different from an uneducated one?

_____

_____

_____

_____

_____

_____

_____

_____

_____

_____

_____

_____

_____

3. Censorship is the practice of keeping certain ideas or pictures out of books, newspapers and magazines, or radio and TV programs. Do you think that governments should ever practice censorship under any circumstances? If so, when, or under what conditions?

_____

_____

_____

_____

_____

_____

_____

_____

_____

_____

_____

_____

_____

_____

4. Although scientists are not sure exactly when religion began, they know that it has existed for over 5,000 years. Explain what religion is and describe the differences between religious and nonreligious people.

_____

_____

_____

_____

_____

_____

_____

_____

_____

_____

_____

_____

5. Some businesses and government agencies regularly test their workers for drug abuse. Do you think this policy is fair? Why or why not?

_____

_____

The Posttest

The posttest test in this chapter will help you decide what writing skills you have learned and what skills you still need to work on.

THE SKILLS BEING TESTED: Like the diagnostic chapter at the beginning of the book, this chapter has three tests.

- The first test is for beginners, or those who are still using the first part of the book. It shows if you can write clearly. This test is not like the GED.

- The second test is for those who have finished the first part of the book and want to know which chapters to do in the second part. It shows if you can write on a topic of general interest. In this test, you will try to support your opinions with good examples and reasons. This test is not timed.

- The third test shows if you are ready for the GED. When you do this test, you will complete your essay in 45 minutes, the time given for the GED.

Remember that the appearance of your paper does not count, as long as your teacher or the tester can read the essay without any trouble. Remember, too, that the tester will not lower your rating if he or she disagrees with your point of view.

RATING THE TEST: After you have taken the test, rate it in the same way as the diagnostic test. That is, mark each skill with a 3, 2, or 1. A 3 means that you have learned the skill. A 2 means that you have started to learn the skill, but need some more practice. A 1 means that you have not yet started to learn the skill. Give yourself an overall score that shows how well your whole essay expresses your point of view.

HOW MUCH HAVE YOU LEARNED: Now compare your essays with those you wrote for the diagnostic test. How many skills have you improved? How many do you need to practice?

WHAT TO DO NEXT: Review the chapters you need to practice. First, read the PREVIEW exercises over again, so you can see what your paragraphs or essays should be like. Second, read the steps or hints for each exercise in the chapter. Then do any problems that are still undone. Lastly, edit the paragraphs or essays you wrote for these chapters; see how much you can improve your own writing.

POSTTEST I

Directions: Write an essay that answers the question below. The essay can be as long or as short as you want.

Question: Almost half of the students in many cities never finish high school. Why do so many students drop out of school? What can be done to keep these students in school?

SKILLS	YOUR SCORE	CHAPTER
a. Main idea		
answers the question	_____	2 & 3
is clearly stated	_____	3
b. Details		
are about the main idea	_____	3 & 5
do not repeat the same ideas	_____	4
c. Organization		
ideas in order	_____	5 & 6
good conclusion	_____	7 & 8
good introduction	_____	8
d. Writing		
correct sentences	_____	9, 10, 11 & 12
separate paragraphs	_____	10, 11 & 12
OVERALL SCORE	_____	

POSTTEST II

Directions: Write a 200-word essay that answers the question below. Take as much time as you want.

Question: The number of Americans who are poor or homeless is growing every year. Explain whether or not you think the nation is doing enough to help these people. Give specific reasons or examples for your point of view.

SKILLS	YOUR SCORE	CHAPTER
a. Main Idea		
answers the question	_____	2 & 3
is clearly stated	_____	3
b. Details		
are about the main idea	_____	3 & 5
do not repeat the same ideas	_____	4
c. Organization		
ideas in order	_____	5 & 6
good conclusion	_____	7 & 8
good introduction	_____	8
d. Writing		
correct sentences	_____	9, 10, 11 & 12
separate paragraphs	_____	10, 11 & 12

SKILLS	YOUR SCORE	CHAPTER
e. Supporting Ideas		
specific details or examples	_____	14
good reasons	_____	15
informative	_____	
complete	_____	
logical	_____	

Note: A good essay shows that you have mastered the skills above. If you are a *really* good writer, you may support your main idea in one of these ways:

f. Contrast	_____	16
g. Compare	_____	16
h. Refute the opposite point of view	_____	17
OVERALL SCORE	_____	

POSTTEST   III

Directions: Write a 200-word essay that answers the question below. Complete the essay in 45 minutes.

Question: According to most economists, Americans today have more money to spend than they did 20 or 30 years ago. Yet, some studies show that most Americans think that life is getting worse for them and their children. Write a 200-word essay that tells if you think life is getting better or worse as time goes on.

SKILLS	YOUR SCORE	CHAPTER
a. Main Idea		
answers the question	_____	2 & 3
is clearly stated	_____	3
b. Details		
are about the main idea	_____	3 & 5
do not repeat the same ideas	_____	4
c. Organization		
ideas in order	_____	5 & 6
good conclusion	_____	7 & 8
good introduction	_____	8
d. Writing		
correct sentences	_____	9, 10, 11 & 12
separate paragraphs	_____	10, 11 & 12

SKILLS	YOUR SCORE	CHAPTER
e. Supporting ideas		
specific details or	_____	14
examples		
good reasons	_____	15
informative		
complete		
logical		

Note: A good essay shows that you have mastered the skills above. If you are a *really* good writer, you may support your main idea in one of these ways:

f.	Contrast	_____	16
g.	Compare	_____	16
h.	Refute the opposite point of view	_____	17
i.	Completed task in time	_____	18
	OVERALL SCORE	_____	

Appendix   1

More Practice GED Questions

1. In his inaugural speech, President John F. Kennedy said, "Ask not what your country can do for you. Ask what you can do for your country." What do you think people should do for their country? Explain why.

2. What is the greatest achievement you or someone you know has made? Why is this achievement so great?

3. According to a 1990 study, people from 18 to 28 years of age care less about the world around them than young adults in the past. "Today's young adult," said the report, "knows less, cares less, votes less and is less critical of its leaders and institutions." Do you think the young adults of today really do care less? Why or why not?

4. Explain the meaning of the old saying, "better safe than sorry." Tell why you agree or disagree with this saying.

5. According to the Declaration of Independence, every American has the right to "life, liberty, and the pursuit of happiness." Do you think our country gives every person that right? Why or why not?

6. Do you think the use of violence is ever justified? Why or why not?

7. One 1990 study showed that American high schools are not giving young people the skills they need in the workplace. Do you agree with this study? Why or why not?

8. People who fail to get what they want most out of life often claim that they are the victims of bad luck. Yet, many successful people say that they had no more luck than anyone else. How important is luck in getting what you want out of life? Explain why you think the way you do.

9. One political writer said that the most important job of government is to help the country's "poor and defenseless" people. Do you agree with this statement? Why or why not?

10. Every person has to make important choices which affect the rest of his or her life. What are the most important choices people make in life? Can they undo these choices, once they are made?

Appendix 2

Model Compositions
and Answer Key

Chapter 2

EXERCISE A: 1-Y; 2-Y; 3-N
EXERCISE C: 1-Y; 2-N; 3-Y; 4-N

Chapter 3

EXERCISE A: a-Y; b-N; c-Y; d-Y
EXERCISE C: 1-Y; 2-Y; 3-N

Chapter 4

EXERCISE A

bank teller—pleasant place

1. A <u>bank teller</u> works in a <u>pleasant place</u>.

medic—keeps patients alive

2. A <u>medic keeps patients alive</u> on the way to the hospital.

park ranger—explains nature

3. A <u>park ranger explains nature</u> to people.

truck drivers—travel, country

4. Most <u>truck drivers travel</u> all over the country.

EXERCISE C

1. I would like to be a house painter. This job is good for me me because I like working by myself and I like making things beautiful. Another reason why I would like to be a house painter is that I could listen to my radio all day while I worked.

1. House painter
   working by myself
   making things beautiful
   listen to radio

2. I would like to be a teacher. One reason that teaching would be good for me is that I like helping people. Another reason is that teachers get a long summer vacation. A third reason is that teachers get a lot of respect.

2. Teacher
   helping people
   long summer vacation
   respect

3. I would like to fix cars. First, I am good with my hands. Second, I love all kinds of cars, especially sports cars. Third, people who fix cars get good pay.

3. Fix cars
   good with my hands
   love cars—especially sports cars
   good pay

Chapter 5

EXERCISE A

1. City Living

   a. Disadvantages
      smog
      crime
      heavy traffic
   b. Advantages
      many movies and comedy clubs
      different kinds of jobs
      good shopping malls

2. Changes Caused by Technology

   a. Home
      VCRs
      compact disk players
      microwave ovens
   b. Business
      fax machines
      office computers

EXERCISE B

1. Having Your Own Business

   a. Advantages
      give people you know jobs
      decide where and when to work
   b. Disadvantages
      no job benefits
      need money to start out
      lose money if business fails

2. Modern Problems

   a. Pollution
      dirty water
      smog
      acid rain
      oil spills
   b. Poverty
      homelessness
      hunger
      not enough good jobs

3. Job of a Parent

   a. Keep child healthy
      feed child healthful foods
      keep child warm in winter
      give child a place to sleep
      take child for checkups at the doctor's
   b. Make sure child is happy
      listen to child's problems
      play games with child
   c. Teach child
      teach child what is right and wrong
      help child with homework

Chapter 6

EXERCISE A

Question 1:   2, 1, 3
Question 2:   3, 1, 2

EXERCISE B

1. MODEL NOTES
   1-slept late
   2-met new friends
   3-went swimming
   2-shared food with friends
   1-took a nap every afternoon

1. Rest
   slept late
   took naps every afternoon
2. New friends
   shared food
3. Swimming

1. MODEL ESSAY

The best vacation I had was the time I went camping with my friends. The <u>main</u> reason we had such a good time is that we just rested. We all slept late and took a nap every afternoon.

<u>A second reason</u> why I enjoyed my camping vacation so much was that I made friends with the campers in the site next to ours. Although these campers were about ten years older than me and my friends, the two groups hit it off right away. We shared food and listened to tapes together. At the end of the week, we exchanged telephone numbers and even made plans to visit each other.

<u>A third</u> reason why I had such a good time was the lake on the campgrounds. Although it rained several times during the week, my friends and I managed to swim at least once a day.

Notice: The writer "brainstormed" the answer before writing the essay.

2. MODEL ESSAY

The main change I would make as office boss is to tell everyone to sign in their work hours. In our office, many workers don't work as long as they are supposed to. As a result, we never get enough work done.

Another important change would be to stop the night janitors from stealing. Everyone complains because things disappear from their desks at night. The boss should change cleaning companies or call the police.

Finally, I would also put a microwave in the lunchroom. Most workers would like hot lunches, but these lunches cost too much to buy. A microwave would let us heat soups and leftovers from home.

Notice: What notes might the writer have used for this essay?

Chapter 7

EXERCISE A

Question 1:   1-SU; 2-SO; 3-F
Question 2:   1-SU; 2-F or SO

Chapter 8

EXERCISE A

1.   Introduction–b; Body–a,c; Summary Conclusion–d

2.   Introduction–c; Body–d,b; Future Conclusion–a

EXERCISE B

1. MODEL INTRODUCTION: People are not doing enough to solve the problem of pollution. Our water and air are getting dirtier, not cleaner, every year.

MODEL BODY: People have not stopped our waters from being polluted. We still have oil spills like the 1989 oilspill in Alaska. Many beaches are so unclean that swimmers cannot use them.

Air pollution is getting worse too. In the last ten years, many cities have passed laws to reduce the pollution from cars. However, car fumes still poison our air. In fact, some scientists claim that the temperature around the world is getting hotter because of air pollution.

MODEL SUMMARY CONCLUSION: In summary, water and air pollution are getting worse. Most people admit that pollution is a problem, but they are not doing enough to solve it.

MODEL SOLUTION CONCLUSION: In conclusion, our government needs to fight harder against pollution. First, we should make people who pollute the air pay heavy fines. Second, we should have more educational programs that tell how to keep our world clean.

MODEL FUTURE CONCLUSION: If people don't work harder to solve the pollution problem, we will spoil the world we live in. The longer we wait, the harder it will be to make our world clean again. In fact, it might even be too late.

2. MODEL ESSAY

Some people say that "Two heads are better than one." This saying means that two people can solve more problems and come up with better ideas than one person.

For example, two people can start a business more easily than one. When the work is divided between two people, each person can do the job he or she likes best. The partner who likes math may keep track of the money and the partner who likes working with people may manage the workers and talk to the customers. Sharing the work helps each partner enjoy the work and do a better job.

If more people realized that two heads are better than one, we might solve more problems and fight less, too.

Chapter 9

Answers to subject/verb exercises

a-1 subject: dealer	verb: will sell
a-2 subject: workers	verb: must take
a-3 subject: people	verb: live
b-1 subjects: someone, who	verbs: plays, will be
c-1 subjects: we, you	verbs: will do, say

d-1 subjects: restaurant, I   verbs: is, will get
e-1a subject: I   verb: will find
e-1b subjects: I, knew   verbs: will find, starts
e-2c subject: landlord   verb: raised
e-2d subjects: landlord, taxes   verbs: raised, were increased

EXERCISE A

1-Fragment; Model Sentence– I will be on vacation for one week.

2-Sentence

3-Fragment; Model Sentence– The gardener begins selling plants as soon as spring arrives.

4-Sentence

5-Fragment; Model Sentence– The workers asked for help, although they knew how to do the job.

6-Fragment; Model Sentence– The package labels will help me decide which foods are most healthful.

EXERCISE B

1. Most citizens vote, pay taxes, and obey their country's rules, even though they may not agree with every action their government takes.

2. Smart people may not know how to read and write well, but they can solve difficult problems.

3. Television encourages you to read by making you interested in the different places and people shown on the screen.

4. City air can cause breathing problems because of the fumes from cars and factories.

EXERCISE C

1-Run-on; Model Sentence- Learn to fly after you join the airforce.

2-Correct Sentence

3-Run-on; Model Sentence- I will watch TV when my favorite program is on.

4-Run-on; Model Sentence- No one said a word because everyone was waiting for the news program to begin.

5-Correct Sentence

6-Correct Sentence

EXERCISE D

1. *Sentence Pair:* Firefighters work long hours. They often face danger to save people.
   Connected Sentence: Firefighters work long hours and often face danger to save people.

2. *Sentence Pair:* Computers are increasingly used at home and in the office. They can do a variety of tasks such as word processing.
   Connected Sentence: Computers are increasingly used at home and in the office because they can do a variety of tasks such as word processing.

3. *Sentence Pair:* Our country has so many different problems. People cannot decide which problems are most important and should be solved first.
   Connected Sentence: Our country has so many different problems that people cannot decide which problems are most important and should be solved first.

4. *Sentence Pair:* Writing skills are necessary to communicate with people who are far away. They are also necessary to keep records of important events.
   Connected Sentence: Writing skills are necessary to communicate with people who are far away and to keep records of important events.

EXERCISE E

1. *Question:* There is an old saying, "Blood is thicker than water." Explain what this saying means.
   Paragraph: The saying "Blood is thicker than water" means that family ties are stronger than the ties of friends. Because people in a family have known each other and lived in the same house since childhood, we say they are of the same 'blood.' When sorrow strikes a person, other members of that family almost feel as though they themselves have been struck.

2. *Question:* Many patriots show their love for their country by saying. "My country, right or wrong." Explain what this expression means and whether you agree with it.
   Paragraph: "My country, right or wrong" means that citizens should support their country, even though it has many faults. For example, the United States has many problems, such as racism and poverty. Just the same, it is still the best country in which to live. When citizens who love their country feel sad about all its problems, they should work hard to correct what is wrong.

Chapter 10

EXERCISE B

1. MODEL ESSAY:

A friend is someone for whom you have a special feeling and who has a special feeling for you in return.

First, friends share their troubles. When you have a problem, a friend never laughs at you; instead, the friend will help you figure out what to do.

Friends are also important because they like to do the same things you do, such as watching sports on TV, fixing up old cars, or listening to rock music. In fact, almost anything you do is more fun with a friend.

These are just two examples of ways in which friends are important. Not everyone likes to do the same things that you like or takes the time to help you solve a problem. That's why a friend is so special.

2. MODEL ESSAY:

People often say, "Pride goeth before a fall." This saying means that some people think that they cannot make a mistake. As a result, they become careless and fail.

One example of a proud person headed for a fall is the boss who does not listen to the opinions of the other workers. In the end, such bosses may make mistakes that could have been avoided had they talked to others.

Another example that shows the truth of this saying is that of a football team after it has won a game. The players on the team might begin to think they are really great, especially if their opponents have a good reputation. The players may decide they don't have to practice for the next game. In the end, the team may lose, simply because it was not prepared.

In conclusion, to avoid a fall, people should listen to others and never be unprepared.

Chapter 11

EXERCISE A:

Question 1 Final copy

The court should have allowed the woman to be a Boy Scout leader. First, Boy Scouts should respect all people, whether they are male or female. Secondly, many young boys today don't have the chance to be around older people, since their grandparents often live in another city. By having an older woman as a leader, these boys will learn that older people have many special qualities. Thirdly, boys should learn that women as well as men can be good leaders. In summary, having a 67-year-old woman as a leader would have helped the Boy Scouts understand and appreciate people who are not like themselves.

Notice: In what two places is the writer's point of view stated more clearly? What sentence has been erased?

Question 2 Final copy

When historians say that history repeats itself, they mean that the same events often happen over and over again. For example, stronger countries have attacked weaker countries in the past, just as they do in modern times. Also, many nations become powerful and then fall apart. This happened to Rome almost two thousand years ago and then it happened to the British Empire in this century. In summary, history doesn't change because people and nations behave in the same way now as they did thousands of years ago.

Notice: Where is the writer's point of view more clearly stated? What sentence has been erased?

EXERCISE B

Question 1 Final copy

Wild animals should be left undisturbed in their natural habitat. First and most importantly, if all the animals are captured and put in zoos, scientists will not be able to study their natural behavior. Second, keeping animals in zoos is unfair to the animals themselves. Many zoo animals are not healthy because zookeepers cannot feed them foods found in woods and jungles. Also, zoo animals are often unhappy because they cannot roam free. To summarize, wild animals are more useful to scientists, as well as being healthier and happier, than zoo animals.

Notice: Which extra words and sentences have been eliminated? Why were the words "most importantly" added?

Question 2 Final copy

Our country is better because it has more senior citizens than ever before. First, because senior citizens often have extra time, they may be more willing to do volunteer work. In fact, many cities already use senior citizens to tutor children in schools, cook meals for shelters, or work in libraries. Thus, many senior citizens are setting good examples for how to grow older and still remain useful.

Notice: What words have been erased? Which sentence has been changed and moved?

EXERCISE C:

Question 1 Final copy

"For every cloud there is a silver lining" means that every problem has a bright side. For example, people who lose their jobs often feel hopeless; however, the chance to find a new and better job is like the silver lining in the cloud. In fact, some studies have shown that many successful people are those who have failed in school or business and then tried again. The lessons these people learned are the "silver lining" because these lessons helped people succeed in the end.

Notice: What words and sentences have been erased? Why? What writing mistakes have been corrected?

Question 2 Final copy

I disagree with President Reagan's statement that people who are hungry just don't know where to go. First, some people, especially those in rural areas, don't live near places that give out food. Second, others are too old or sick to go to food centers. In summary, many people are still hungry in our country because they can't get to food centers.

Notice: What two ideas are combined into one sentence? In what two places is the writer's point of view more clearly stated?

Chapter   12

EXERCISE A: *Question 1*

MODEL ESSAY: YES

People who cheat on an important test should be expelled from school.

First, students who cheat are not interested in learning but in getting a passing grade. Such students may be taking the place of other students who want to learn.

Second, students who cheat in school are likely to continue cheating once they graduate and get a job. If the school doesn't teach them be honest now, they may learn the hard way—by getting fired from their job.

Third, if students who cheat are not expelled, everyone in the class suffers because the grades given for tests and papers are worthless. No one will know which students cheated and which students really earned their grades.

In conclusion, allowing cheating harms both the cheaters and the other students in the school. Therefore, cheaters should receive a harsh punishment for their actions.

MODEL ESSAY: NO

Although all students who cheat on an important test should be punished, only some should be expelled from school.

First, alternate punishments for first-time cheaters might be more appropriate. For example, these students could either retake the test or be suspended, rather than expelled, from school. Such students may learn their lesson and never cheat again.

A second reason for giving cheaters another chance is that they may be having trouble learning. The best way to stop such people from cheating is to offer them special help, either before or after classes.

Third, those who want to expel cheaters from school should keep in mind what such a severe punishment might mean to the individual student. Students who are expelled may be so bitter they will never attend school again. Furthermore, they might lose their job if their employer found out that they were dishonest. Therefore, expulsion from school should be used only when the student has cheated at least once and been warned of what the punishment may be.

In summary, people who cheat should be given different punishments, depending on the circumstances.

Question 2

MODEL ESSAY: YES

People should be put in jail, even if they are stealing because they are hungry.

No one has to steal in order to eat. Most poor people can get either food stamps for the supermarket or food from a shelter or a church set up for that purpose.

If people who steal food to survive were not put in jail, all thieves would say they were hungry, a claim that would be hard to disprove. The possibility of escaping punishment would cause even more people to steal.

In conclusion, hungry people can get food without stealing. If we do not put hungry people in jail for stealing food, we will cause more crime.

MODEL ESSAY: NO

People who steal when they are hungry should not be put in jail. First, these people probably would not steal if they had food to eat. Instead of spending the money to keep them in jail, society should give them food and help them find a job. This solution is more merciful and permanent than punishing someone who steals out of need rather than choice.

Second, imprisoning people who steal food when they are hungry may cause them to become criminals. They would learn from the criminals around them how to pick locks and snatch purses. Then our country would have more criminals, not less.

Third, our jails are overcrowded already. Therefore, we should imprison only those who are a real danger to others. By letting hungry people take up jail space, we may be forced to let other, more violent criminals out on the streets.

In conclusion, a person who steals because of hunger should be helped, rather than jailed. Offering these people food and help in finding jobs would be best for them and best for society.

EXERCISE B

1. MODEL ESSAY: YES

Women should be forced to serve in the military during a war, just as men are.

First, drafting women in wartime is fair to both women and men. Now that women have the same rights as men, they should have the same duties, no matter how dangerous those duties are.

Second, a draft that does not include women is unfair to our whole nation. Over half of our adult citizens are women. Why should the country be cheated of the talents and skills that these citizens have to offer?

Third, women are better able to do different jobs in the military than they were twenty years ago. For example, many women today are doctors, pilots, and scientists. If women have the same jobs as men in peacetime, they should have the same jobs in wartime as well.

No one hopes for another war such as the one in Vietnam. However, if one should arise, our nation should be able to use all its citizens. The idea of women soldiers may seem strange at first, but in modern times women can, and should, serve on an equal basis.

MODEL ESSAY: NO

Women should not be forced to serve in the armed forces during a war.

First, women may be just as smart as men, but they are not as strong. Therefore, the enemy might find it easier to fight and conquer a military force that has women in it—especially in situations involving physical combat.

Second, women are not as used to violence as men. When heavy fighting begins, the women might break down or refuse to fight, leaving the men to defend the women as well as themselves.

Third, having women work so closely with males in the military might cause arguments among the troops themselves. Far away from home and from their loved ones, many men might forget that the women near them should be regarded only as fighting partners. The men might begin fighting amongst themselves about which woman "belongs" to which man. These arguments destroy the trust that is so necessary for a fighting force to be effective.

In conclusion, women may be just as able to do many jobs as men. However, they are not as able to fight well and their presence might cause men to fight less effectively too.

Chapter   13

EXERCISE A

A factory has to let some workers go. Which workers should they fire—those who were the last to get hired or those who don't do good work?

Me: The factory should fire the workers who were the last to get hired. Many of these workers are younger and don't need the money as much as the older workers do. Also, younger workers can find a job more easily than older workers can.

Other person: The factory should let the best workers stay and fire the rest. The workers who do a good job help the factory more than those who don't. Those who need the money the most are probably the ones who work the hardest, too.

EXERCISE B

MODEL PARAGRAPH: YES

We should let more immigrants come to our country to live. First, America is the richest country in the world; we have enough money and jobs in our country to help others. Second, the family of every American today—except the Indians—came from somewhere else; by letting more immigrants in we are giving them the same chance to be happy we or our ancestors had.

MODEL PARAGRAPH: NO

Too many people want to come to America. If we let in all those people, we won't have anything left for ourselves. When immigrants come here to live and work, they take away jobs Americans want to have. Also, sometimes we have to pay for their food and clothing because they come without anything at all. Instead of paying for immigrants to come and live here, we should give the jobs and the money to the poor people who are already here.

Chapter 14

EXERCISE A

1. *Washington, D.C.* has no representatives in Congress because it is not part of a state or a territory.

2. A New York City study estimated that *over 500 homeless* people live in Grand Central station.

3. Skills *such as word processing* are becoming more and more needed *in the job market.*

4. *Most* jobs require their employees to work *seven or eight hours* a day.

5. Many companies have *dental and medical* insurance plans for *all* their employees.

EXERCISE B

1. TV programs such as those produced by National Geographic are more educational than other kinds.

2. The parents usually make the most important decisions in a family.

3. If you cut yourself, put iodine or an antibiotic ointment on the wound.

4. Most TV commercials are only one or two minutes long.

5. Problems such as drug abuse and crime seem impossible for cities to solve.

EXERCISE C

MODEL PARAGRAPH:

High school sports such as football can be dangerous. Every year, about two dozen high school students die from football injuries. Many need operations on their knees. Young football players may be sorry later on that they played.

EXERCISE D

1. War is the worst problem the world faces today. This problem has been going on for thousands of years—even before history began. Every year, war kills or cripples thousands of civilians and leaves thousands more starving or homeless. Whole villages in countries such as Vietnam have been destroyed by war. Although organizations such as the United Nations have been established to stop war, people keep on fighting each other.

EXERCISE E

1. MODEL PARAGRAPH: YES

Burning the American flag should be allowed; it is a constitutional right, just like freedom of speech. Our Constitution says Americans have the right to show that they disagree with the government, as long as they don't cause a riot. If we take away the right to burn the flag, we may take away other constitutional rights that have kept our country free for over 200 years.

MODEL PARAGRAPH: NO

People should not have the right to burn the flag, even when they disagree with the actions of its leaders. Because the flag is the symbol of our country, treating it with disrespect is like treating the whole country with disrespect. Furthermore, thousands of soldiers have died in wars for over two hundred years to defend the flag; burning it is like telling their families that these soldiers died for nothing. In summary, people may make speeches against national actions they do not like, but they should not be allowed to insult the country as a whole.

EXERCISE F

Big cities have many problems such as poverty, overcrowding, and pollution.

Although most city governments have programs that help the poor, the number of people who cannot afford to house or feed themselves is growing. This causes a problem for everyone because more and more tax dollars are needed to support those who cannot support themselves.

Second, the cities are getting too crowded. Often, they do not have enough housing. Also, they just cannot afford to give so many people services such as street cleaning or hospital care.

Third, pollution caused by car fumes is getting worse. Cities need to control pollution by having stricter laws against car fumes and better public transportation.

Today, many who can afford a home in the suburbs are leaving the city. If the cities can't solve their problems within the next few years, no one will be left but those who have no choice—the poor.

EXERCISE G

If I won a million dollars, I would change my life in several ways.

First, I would use the money to fulfill a dream I've had for over 5 years—start my own grocery store. In addition to fresh produce and the usual packaged foods, I would also sell homemade salads and pastries that my mother and aunt make.

Second, I would move to a house near Sutton St. My new house would have more rooms; I would even have a special room for a pool table.

Even though I had a million dollars however, I would keep some of the things in my life the same. For example, I wouldn't change my dog, even though I got her from the SPCA and she isn't worth any money. Also, I wouldn't change my friends because we have such a good time together.

Chapter 15

EXERCISE A: 1-b; 2-b; 3-a; 4-b; 5-a.

EXERCISE B: 1-a; 2-b; 3-b; 4-a; 5-b.

EXERCISE C: 1-b; 2-a; 3-a; 4-b; 5-b.

EXERCISE D

1. Having basic math skills is important because these skills are needed for everyday tasks such as balancing a checkbook or calculating a bill.

2. Computers are becoming more popular because they are cheaper and easier to use than before.

3. People should save as much as they can because they might need the money for an emergency.

4. A strong national army is important because it will prevent other countries from attacking us.

EXERCISE E

a. *People should use credit cards.* Credit cards are safer to carry around than money, because card owners can always report a stolen card. Also, credit cards may save money because they enable their owners to buy an item on sale, even if they don't have the cash. These two reasons show why credit cards can be a benfit.

b. *People should not use credit cards.* Many people buy too much with credit cards and then have trouble paying their bills. Also, using credit cards raises prices because stores pay credit card companies a percentage of every purchase made with their cards; the stores then pass this added cost onto the consumer. In summary, credit cards should not be used because they encourage people to borrow too much and because they raise costs.

EXERCISE F

MODEL PARAGRAPH: YES

1. Our justice system is fair to the poor. The Bill of Rights in our Constitution guarantees that all defendants have the same rights in court, no matter how poor or rich they are. For example, the sixth amendment states that the government must provide lawyers for all those who cannot afford legal aid. It also states that all trials must be public, so that the accused person's family and friends can watch and make sure the the court is acting fairly. Furthermore anyone found guilty of a major crime can appeal to a higher court if he or she thinks the verdict or the sentence is unjust.

MODEL PARAGRAPH: NO

Our justice system is not fair to the poor. First, poor people can't afford to pay for the lawyers of their choice the way rich people can. Second, poor people may wind up in jail because they can't pay for bail or for fines. In conclusion, our justice system is unfair to people who don't have the money to hire good lawyers and to pay bail or fines.

EXERCISE G

1. MODEL ESSAY: YES

Citizens who refuse to fight in wartime should be put in jail. First, our nation needs the strongest armed forces possible in order to win the war. It needs the help of everyone who is able to fight—even those who would prefer to be at home.

Second, allowing some citizens to stay at home might anger those who are at the front. Whereas those at the front have left their jobs and family to defend our country, many others may be leading a safe and comfortable life—just because they say the war is wrong. Furthermore, those who refuse to fight may be getting all the good jobs left behind and making a lot of money. Rather than being rewarded for their bravery and dedication to their country, those who risked their lives may find they have lost their job when they return.

Third, giving people a choice may cause some to refuse to fight, even if they don't think the war is wrong. Many may say they object to the war simply because they don't want to fight. No one would know who refuse to fight because of selfishness and who because of sincere antiwar feelings.

In summary, giving some citizens the right to refuse serving during wartime is both unfair and harmful to our country. It weakens our armed forces by reducing the number of people who serve and by creating bitterness amongst those who choose to fight.

MODEL ESSAY: NO

Citizens who refuse to fight in wartime should not be put in jail. First, some religions say that people should never kill, even in wartime. By forcing believers in these religions to fight, the country is taking away their right to religious freedom.

Second, people who do not want to fight can do many other kinds of work. These people could tutor children or adults, build homes for the homeless, or even repair roads. By doing these jobs for a low pay, people would save the country money.

Third, those who think a particular war is immoral should be encouraged to act on their conscience and speak their mind. After all, more and more people may agree with their objections in the end. For example, when the war in Vietnam first began, only a few citizens objected. However, as the years went on, more and more people agreed that our country should not be fighting in Southeast Asia. Few young people wanted to fight there, and our country lost several fine citizens who fled to Canada.

In conclusion, people should not be forced to fight in a war they think is wrong. If enough people refuse to fight, the leaders should consider getting out of the war altogether.

Chapter 16

EXERCISE A

The jobs of a supermarket bagger and a mailcarrier are very different. Whereas a bagger works inside the store, a mail carrier usually stays outdoors. Another difference is that unlike a mail carrier, a bagger may have to work in the nighttime or on Sundays when the store is open.

In summary, a supermarket bagger's workplace and hours are different from those of a mail carrier.

Ideas contrasted: job of a supermarket bagger and job of a mailcarrier. Clue words: *different, whereas, unlike*

EXERCISE B

1. Life today is different from the life my parents had forty years ago. Unlike most families of forty years ago, many families of today do not live together. Forty years ago, grandparents, parents, and children often lived in the same town or even in the same house. In contrast, today older people are put into nursing homes. Younger people move to cities where they can get the best jobs, no matter how far away these cities are from their parents. Although modern families talk to each other on the phone and visit each other as often as possible, they are not as close as they used to be.

EXERCISE C

The jobs of a supermarket bagger and mailcarrier are alike in many ways. The bagger often has to lift and carry heavy bags of groceries. Similarly, a mailcarrier has to carry heavy bags of mail. Also, both a bagger and a mailcarrier wear uniforms.

Ideas compared: job of a supermarket bagger and job of a mailcarrier. Clue words: *alike, similarly, both*

EXERCISE D

1. In many ways, I have not changed in the last ten years. I still play basketball every Saturday, just as I did then. Similarly, some of my dreams have not changed. Ten years ago I decided that I would earn enough money to help my parents move to a better home. I still hope that someday I will make that dream come true.

2. In some ways, life is the same today as it was forty years ago. The cities of today are still overcrowded and full of poor people, just as they were forty years ago. Like the voters of today, voters forty years ago did not want to pay taxes to help the poor and homeless. The people of both generations seem to have learned little about solving important problems.

EXERCISE E

The jobs of a supermarket bagger and a mailcarrier are both alike and different. The bagger often lifts and carries heavy bags of groceries. In the same way, the mailcarrier often lifts and carries heavy bags. On the other hand, the supermarket bagger often has to work in the late evenings and on Sundays, whereas the mailcarrier does not.

Compared: *alike, in the same way*

Contrasted: *different, on the other hand, whereas*

EXERCISE F

Same: give best workers biggest Christmas bonuses

Different: hire more trained mechanics
        close on Sundays

If I were the manager of the garage where I work, I would change some policies and keep others. Whereas my manager keeps only two trained mechanics, I would have at least three or four, so the customers would not have to wait too long for their cars. Unlike my manager, too, I would close the garage on Sundays, because too few customers come on that day. One policy I would keep is to give the best workers the biggest Christmas bonuses. Thus, if I ran our garage, the customers would be happier because they would get better service and the workers would be happier because they would work better hours and would get paid fairly.

EXERCISE G

Same: cook for family
       raise children

Different: work outside home
          different jobs—firefighting, police, truck driving

The role of women today is both the same as and different from the way it was forty years ago.

Most women today have the same responsibilities at home as women had over forty years ago. Like their mothers and grandmothers before them, most modern women still cook for their families and raise their children, while their husbands fix the car or an electrical appliance.

On the other hand, unlike most women of forty years ago, most women today also work outside the home. In addition to their family responsibilities, they often have fulltime jobs. Furthermore, women's careers are very different from those of forty years ago, when most people used to think that women should be teachers, nurses, and secretaries. Today, many women have careers in jobs such as firefighting, police work, and even truck driving.

Some women like the changes in their roles and hope for even more changes in the future. Others think that modern women have lost their special role as caring mother and wife and are trying too hard to be like men.

Chapter 17

EXERCISE A

MODEL PARAGRAPH: YES

Educating young people about the dangers of drugs is not the best way to reduce drug abuse right now. Although education has a more lasting effect than any other solution, it will not solve the immediate problem of getting drug dealers off the streets. Nor will it persuade those who are already addicts to quit their habit. If everyone who abused or sold drugs were put in jail, the rest of the people might be afraid to get involved too.

MODEL PARAGRAPH: NO

Many people think the government could reduce the use of illegal drugs by putting more drug abusers and dealers in jail. However, if every abuser or dealer were jailed, our prisons would be so overcrowded that we would have to let some criminals go free. Therefore, we should spend the money to educate young people about the dangers of drugs. Although this solution would take more time it would have a lasting effect. Illegal drugs would simply disappear from our streets because no one would want them any more.

EXERCISE B

MODEL PARAGRAPH: YES

I agree with the saying "cream rises to the top." Some may argue that people may fail because of bad luck or because they made one bad decision. On the other hand, those who really have the ability to succeed will not let one failure stop them forever. These people will learn from their mistakes and try again. If necessary, they may try several times, until at last they succeed.

MODEL PARAGRAPH. NO

The saying "cream rises to the top" is often true. For example, people who are hard workers and who are well educated have a better chance of succeeding than those who are not. Yet, many people fail, despite their efforts and their skills. For example, people may fail in business because of a recession or because they made one wrong decision. In conclusion, people who "rise to the top" are not necessarily better than those who have failed.

EXERCISE C

ESSAY: YES

All women with babies should go back to work if they want to. Women should have the same rights to work or to stay at home as men do.
Some people argue that mothers of young children should work only if they need the money. Yet, each family should be able to decide for itself what is "enough money."
Other people argue that children with mothers at home are happier than the children of working mothers. However, caring for a child at home does not guarantee that the child will be better adjusted. In fact, many children whose mothers stay at home do not grow up to be well-adjusted.
In conclusion, every mother should decide for herself what is best for her and her children.

ESSAY: NO

All women with babies should not go back to work. They should stay at home and care for their babies for at least a few years.
Some people argue that some mothers cannot afford to stay at home while their babies are young. However, the well-being of a woman's family is more important than any money she could earn.
Other people argue that each mother should decide for herself what is best for her and her family. This argument ignores the fact that all babies have the same need: one person who can care for them when they are sick and play with them when they are well. No one can do that job as well as a mother can.
In summary, caring for a baby is a fulltime job. Therefore, all mothers should not work outside the home until their babies are older.

EXERCISE D

MODEL ESSAY: YES

Governments should use capital punishment as a punishment for some murders. Too often, violent criminals escape from jail and then commit the same crimes.
Some people argue that capital punishment is unfair because most people executed are poor. However, middle-class and wealthy murderers have been sentenced to death, too. Accord-

ing to our Constitution, judges should think only of the crime committed, not how poor or rich the criminal is.

Another argument against capital punishment is that the wrong person may be executed. Yet, most judges give the death penalty only when they and the jury are sure that the suspect is guilty. Furthermore, convicted murderers often get their death sentences overturned by a higher court.

In conclusion, capital punishment is a fair way to keep convicted murderers off the streets.

MODEL ESSAY: NO

We should never punish criminals by killing them, even when they have committed a horrible crime.

Many people think that executing murderers saves money. Yet, convicted murderers often try for years to get death sentence changed. The cost to the court system is often greater than the cost of keeping them in jail.

Many people also think that capital punishment prevents people from committing murder. If this were true, the states having the death penalty would have fewer murders. However, states that have executed murderers in the past 10 years have just as many murders as other states.

Remember, we cannot bring back to life again those whom we have unjustly killed. Society should think of other ways to punish murderers.

EXERCISE E

MODEL ESSAY: YES

Athletes should be admitted to college even if they have low grades or SAT scores.

The National Collegiate Athletic Association claims that these athletes are taking up the space of others who can do college work better. However, most of these other students come from richer homes and have had better chances to get a good education. Furthermore, education does not mean as much to these students as it does to the athletes for whom college is the only escape from the poverty of their parents.

Another argument against admitting athletes with low SAT scores or grades is that many of them never finish college. This argument shows the need for giving these students help with their work, rather than keeping them out altogether. For example, special tutoring classes and basic English and math courses could be set up to help athletes, as well as other students who cannot keep up with their classmates.

Although the main job of a college is to educate, both alumni and students often take pride in the athletics teams. In order to keep the athletic spirit alive, we should get the best athletes possible.

ESSAY: NO

I agree with the National Collegiate Athletic Association that high school athletes should be accepted into college if they have a satisfactory grade point average and SAT score.

Many athletes who did not do well in high school argue that the reason they do poorly on tests is that they have not had the same educational opportunities as other students. Yet, one cause for their poor education might be that they spent too much time on sports and not enough on their studies. If they went to college, they would probably continue to neglect their studies.

Another argument for admitting these athletes is that many of them will be poor for the rest of their lives if they don't go to college. On the other hand, the NCAA pointed out that about 20% of college athletes such as football players never graduate. Very likely, college did not help these athletes at all.

In conclusion, colleges need to consider students' high school records and test scores, as well as their sports ability. Otherwise, colleges will not be fulfilling their main purpose—education.

2. MODEL ESSAY: YES

The Oregon law saying that people over 80 cannot receive medicaid for some services is fair. Such a law helps the people who have the best chance of getting better.

Critics of such a bill argue that the state is causing some older people who cannot afford medical care to die. However, in reality all states are deciding who shall live and who shall die, just by deciding how to spend its limited supply of money. By not spending more money for free clinics or other types of medical care, the state is deciding that people who need these clinics might die. For example, the fact that the United States has a high infant death rate shows that clinics for pregnant women are needed.

Another argument against the Oregon medicaid law is that the states should provide whatever medical care people need—regardless of the cost. This argument, though, is not practical. The cost of complete medical care for everyone has never been calculated, but most people agrees it would be many billions of dollars. Since most taxpayers want to pay less, few state politicians would favor free care to all citizens.

The Oregon medicaid law is not completely satisfactory. However, it does make sure that the state makes the best use of its funds until free care for everyone can be provided.

MODEL ESSAY: NO

The Oregon law saying that people over 80 cannot receive medicaid for some services is not fair.

Those in favor of this law argue that the state needs to spend more money on people who have a better chance to survive. On the other hand, spending money on the health of our senior citizens should not reduce the amount we spend on younger people. In fact, every state should spend as much money as necessary to give all its residents the health care they need.

Another reason why this argument is false is that no one knows how long any patient will survive. For example, many 80-year-olds might have a better chance of surviving major surgery than younger patients with a serious illness.

In conclusion, we do not have the right to keep some people from getting the medical help they need, just because they are older. The Oregon law discriminates against people because of their age by keeping them from getting the same kind of medical care as others.